PASSPORT *to* PARTNERSHIP

Martin Bissett

Sailing Through the Seven Cs to CPA Firm Leadership

Personal Progress Plan & Workbook

PASSPORT TO PARTNERSHIP
MARTIN BISSETT

Published by CPA Trendlines
An imprint of Bay Street Group, LLC
12 Gay Road, #5139
East Hampton, NY 11937 USA

Designed by DittoDoesDesign.com

The research that provides the foundation for this series is being continually carried out with accounting practices ranging from sole practitioners through to top 30 firms in the UK and US as well as central Europe, Canada and the Middle East. This research is ongoing and the results are continually updated.

ISBN: 978-0-9827147-8-2

The author wishes to sincerely thank the following for their support of this project:

Lisa Tierney
Brian Kuczinski
Maureen Renzi
Meg Killian
Sharyne Tromans
M. Scott Myers
Rick Telberg

And all at the Pennsylvania Institute of Certified Public Accountants (PICPA)

How to use this practice manual

Passport to Partnership isn't a book. It's a tool. As such, some operating instructions are in order.

Passport to Partnership is designed to be used by:

1. Individual professionals committed to personal development – working on their own to advance in their skills, their careers, and in their firms and
2. Firms and organizations seeking a comprehensive professional development program – for training, retention and development of key personnel in leadership, client service, practice management, business development, and succession. For the firm, Passport to Partnership provides a platform for supporting partners-in-training, developing talent, positioning a new generation of partner and shareholder, preparing for succession, and for building a sustainable, self-renewing firm for the future.

We suggest users set aside at least 30 minutes at a time, with pencil in hand, to read and review each page, and to perform the exercises. All are important and should be undertaken one step at a time in progressive order. Nothing should be rushed. The seemingly simplest of questions may require the most time and effort.

Passport to Partnership is divided into three parts.

1. The Main section takes users step-by-step through "the seven Cs," which proprietary research and real-world experience show are the keys to success for owners and leaders of many of the world's finest firms.
2. The Personal Progress Plan & Workbook appendix provides a complete set of worksheets forms and checklists, which can be photocopied for convenient use.
3. The Personal Progress Plan & Workbook appendix is also conveniently available as a PDF download, with instructions on page A-1.

Contents

Foreword

Have you ever wondered what the partners of your firm are looking for from you beyond your technical abilities?

For full disclosure, I am not an accountant, but I have spent decades working with accounting firms of all shapes and sizes in the United Kingdom, the United States and Europe.

I noticed over time that in many firms, partners may often regard one or more of their managers as not being 'partner material' because they feel that the manager does not exhibit the traits they are looking for. In turn, the manager is not aware of the traits being sought after by the partners and whilst some of these 'traits' may be just plain common sense, others are not necessarily innate or intrinsic to the individual. That doesn't mean, however, that an individual is incapable of learning them and should be written off.

I became fascinated by this apparent juxtaposition of the partners not vocalising what they were looking for in future partners and the managers not asking, despite wanting to reach that very position. In a profession with a supposed succession crisis on the horizon, this apparent stand-off struck me as curious.

This lead me to personally interview several hundred partners and managers in the US, UK and Europe to learn

1. what the partners are looking for, and

2. how the managers see their own future in the firm.

There are, of course, firms who have addressed this issue already, and their initiatives have also been captured by this research.

The results of the research, including both the consensus and the exceptions to the general opinion, are contained in a series of workshops called Passport to Partnership which are delivered by my company, The Upward Spiral Partnership.

The "Sailing through the seven Cs" program is designed to provide the highlights of each factor employed by the majority of partners interviewed as their criteria for evaluating whether or not someone in their organisation can make it to the top.

I hope you'll join me as we visit each one and I'd be delighted to hear from you if you have further opinion as to anything the conclusions have or haven't shown up thus far. The research is perpetual, and as new findings are established as consensus they will be published here first.

Overview

In this guidebook, you will learn the key characteristics of successful partners. You will also learn how to develop your own personal plan to achieve the level of partnership in your firm. For firms, this guidebook provides a clear set of procedures, processes and milestones for turning top talent into the next generation of firm leadership.

THE SEVEN Cs OF PARTNERSHIP

This refers to your technical abilities and qualifications, whether it be audit abilities, tax computations, or management accounting functionality. Whatever your area of specialism, the partners expect you to be able to know at least as much as anyone else who may report to you.

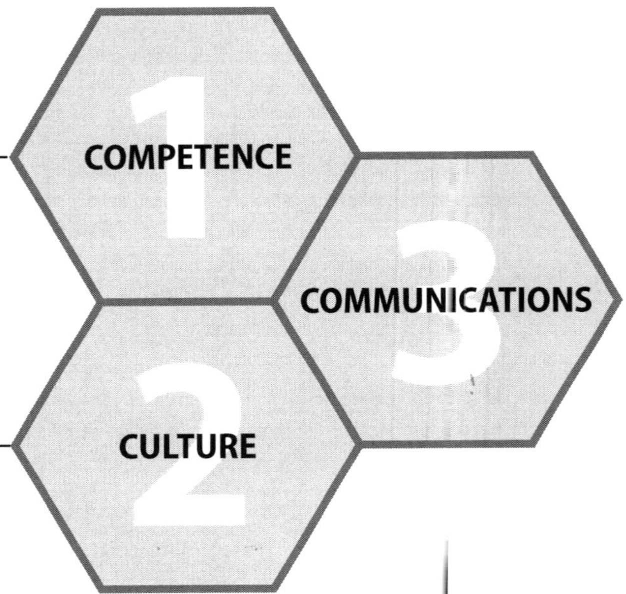

This is your ability to understand why the practice does things the way it does, and the behaviours it expects of its people. It also reflects your ability to be an ambassador for the firm in public.

This includes your internal managerial abilities, external client and 'influencer' relationship building skills, and the discernment to be non-partisan in politically sensitive situations. Basically it's about demonstrating self-assurance without ego.

What happens when a colleague has made a huge mistake and the client is about to find out? Worse still, what happens when that colleague is a partner? What happens when a client needs you now? How you react to challenges says a lot about your maturity and how you would handle firm-wide issues as a partners, given the chances.

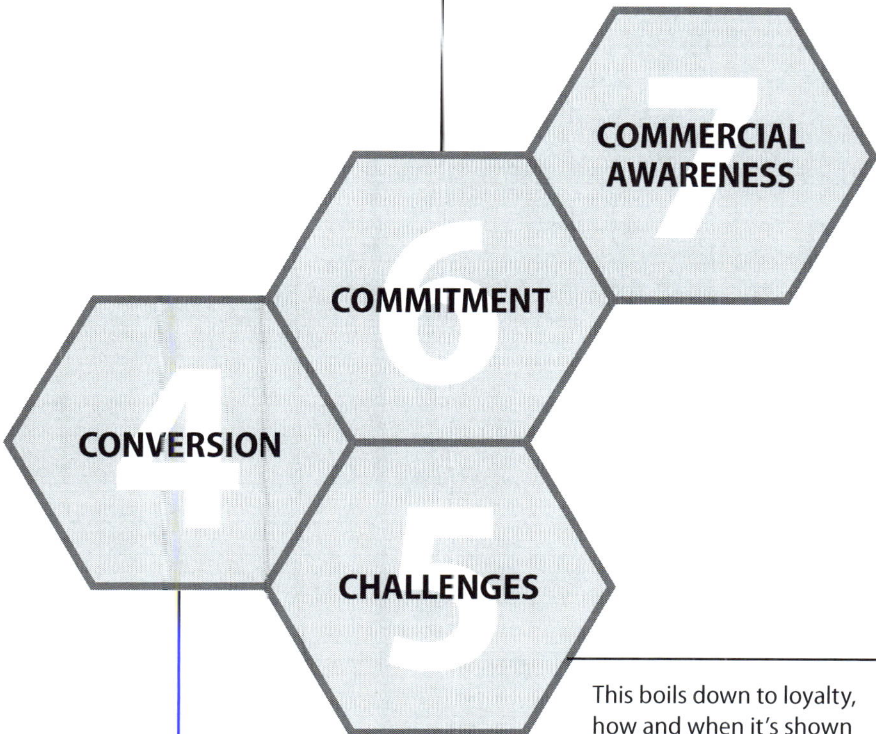

This is the second great attribute of the 21st Century Accountant. Being a competent technician is one thing, but partners are people who run large organisations which just so happen to deliver accounting services. They must deal with issues well beyond accountancy:

- How are we going to meet the payroll this month?
- How do we get all this WIP freed up, billed and collected?
- Why are Johnny and his team running up huge expenses that cut into his department's profitability and bring the whole average down?
- How are this year's figures going to look to the bank when we want to ask them to increase our borrowing to fund the planned expansion?

If you want to become a partner yourself, you must have a commercial awareness of what a partner in your firm actually goes through on a day to day basis.

This boils down to loyalty, how and when it's shown and what happens to a person's career prospects in the firm when it isn't demonstrated at a key time.

This is a major requirement of the 21st century accountant: the ability to source, develop, close and grow a new or existing client relationship. This quality is developed incrementally over time.

Let's get started!

Fill in each section to establish your starting point for career growth.

MY AMBITIONS

What are your career ambitions for the next one to five years?

Earnings ambitions

Life balance ambitions

Type of projects worked on, niche specialisms developed, free time available etc.

Achievements to obtain

Make Partner, start own firm, be recognized for my work, get involved with Charity work etc.

Why do you want to achieve these things specifically?

The most motivational reason is...

The impact of not achieving these things is...

What will you and those closest to you feel like when you've achieved them? How will that day play out?

FINANCIAL OUTLINE

One year from today, what figure would you like your annual salary to have reached?

What is your current salary and how long have you been at that level?

What justification could you give to your firm to support the required increase?

Currently underpaid compared to peer-level elsewhere, in line with rate of inflation, advance against future business brought in etc.

What additional return on investment could you demonstrate to justify the increase?

Extra responsibility, removal of headaches from Partner's workload, self-investment in rainmaking training etc.

Based on these parameters, what do you need to do before you can be successful in achieving this raise?

What areas of weakness have you identified that you need to put right before justifying this raise and what is your plan for doing so and by when?

Overview

The skill in producing financial reports is limited by the quality of the information presented to the CPA by the client. Motivation of the client to influence that financial information comes in many forms, some intentional and some unintentional. Competence comes first in being able to resist pressure and present a true and accurate position of the client's organization.

Sounds obvious, doesn't it? But there's a twist.

Competence didn't actually rank highly in the majority of partner's requirements when interviewed in the study at all. The general view expressed is that technical ability could be 'bought' much easier than some of the other skill sets that they looked for in a potential partner. Many assumed technical competence would be present for someone to even be considered for partnership.

However, where there was a high value placed on technical skills was where the prospective partner brought something to the table that the firm didn't already have at partner level. Whilst this changed from firm to firm, the most common specialisms the partner's desired were forensic accounting abilities and various tax expertise such as international tax and industry-specific knowledge.

Where a senior manager could demonstrate an expert level of knowledge in these fields, the partners 'ticked the first box' in that manager's application for a 'passport to partnership.' As the study has progressed, we've seen that 'competence' has grown from a mere required 'given' that a potential partner would have her or his qualifications and have been practising to a certain degree of experience; through to requiring a more broad and mature leadership competence — the competence to be partner or in other words, to possess as many if not all seven Cs before becoming appointed.

The thing is, we're millennials for the most part. We grew up in the late eighties and through the nineties in times of unparalleled economic prosperity. Many of us had parents who could afford to give us every opportunity to develop as they had done well for themselves. We experienced a technological acceleration which changed communications and opportunity creation forever. We saw no debilitating worldwide conflicts, rationing, requirement for huge self-sacrifice and we had constant and repeated positive feedback to live off.

—

The business landscape, as regards the traits and behaviours, outlooks and attitudes that constitute success, has NOT changed.

That does NOT prepare us for leadership.

The Partners that we aspire to join, take over from, buy out or be granted equity from, had to deal with all of this. They were the baby boomers, the post war recovery era where 'sweat equity' was the minimum amount of investment required just to keep a career on track. They were, according to the passport to partnership survey, rarely if ever in receipt of praise, clear instruction, mapped out career paths or any other 'luxury' that we have the tendency of thinking is our right to receive now.

Therefore 'competence' needs to be re-thought, especially as we will shape our next 'C' – Culture, for a generation even less acquainted with these conditions and requirements than we are.

The business landscape, in as far as what traits and behaviours, outlooks and attitudes constitute success HASN'T changed. So the challenge here then is for us to understand and feel and think like the present leaders of our firm do, but with a modern twist.

How do we do that?

The expert council

Here's what a number of experts exclusively interviewed for this project had to say.

Many young professionals complain of not really understanding what they need to do to make it to partner. What would be your counsel to them?

Well, first of all, I ask them what would it mean to them to be partner? When they are partner, how will it change their overall professional experience? Once we have established WHY they want to be partner, we now have identified the motivators around this goal that we can work toward....we can see it, feel it and understand why it's worth our working toward that goal with small steps.

Lisa Tierney
Tierney Consulting

I would counsel them to take the bull by the horns and work on self-development. Making partner is about becoming an asset to the organization. That doesn't happen by just developing technical skills and it doesn't happen from 9 to 5 M-F. Young professionals wanting to make partner need to be able to lead, manage and develop business and show the firm they are invested. Most of today's partners didn't grow up with a guide book to making partner, which is partially what is so difficult about the current transition CPA firms are facing. Stop waiting for them to hand you something and take the initiative to developing the skills that will position for the role.

Sarah Johnson Dobek
Inovautus Consulting

Unless they want to be a partner to strive to achieve change in the firms they work for, it's easier to do things differently in your own sphere. I'd advise them to document evidence of why things should be done differently because even the most obvious conclusions have to be evidence based in the accounting profession. Otherwise don't be a partner, find your own vision and create your own firm.

Ron Baker CPA
Verasage Institute

The Professional Services market place is going through a period of unprecedented change with pressure from just about every stakeholder – some well-established – such as regulators, clients, professional bodies and others that are starting to show some of their power which is manifested in the way social media is exposing firms , leaders and staff to public scrutiny. In the midst of this the ideal of "partnership" seems to be gaining a resurgence.

So for partners in the 21st Century it is a tough combination. Being technically more than just proficient will get you started, you will need good relationship skills – but built on something in addition to your technical skill set – so an understanding of strategy, business, politics, commerce will be essential. And then add to that a set of leadership skills that enable one to lead diverse, virtual, fragmented groups and bring them together quickly and effectively to solve client's problems. All of this in an unforgiving, global environment that demands flexibility and consistency – which are not mutually exclusive. It is a tall order.

Mike Mister
Global Director of Executive Development
Ernst & Young Global

Case study on Competence

Michael was the 'heir apparent' in his 4 partner firm. He had worked his way up from being a junior on less than $16,000 a year through to being on the verge of Partnership.

Whilst Michael was thought of as being diligent, mature and certainly leadership material, the promise of seniority had also brought a small but growing complacency in his attitude towards clients.

A lazy misjudgment of the urgency of an issue had led to a client losing out on the purchase of a major office development, a client to whom the firm billed over $100,000 a year, and which resulted in a complaint about Michael to the Managing Partner.

Michael found himself in the Managing Partner's office and this time, not for after-work drinks or friendly chit-chat. Rather, Michael was chastised for his laissez-faire attitude.

There is nothing wrong with advising the client that you don't immediately have an answer for them but will investigate and get back to them within an agreed timeframe.

The Managing Partner told him:

You have exhibited a tendency to try and use routine answers for situations you have found yourself in. Although your experience and therefore 'stock' grows over time, you have neither in sufficient quantity to afford yourself the luxury of using them with clients of this firm, especially not ones who it would take us years to replace were we ever to lose them.

You have a need to increase your competence in a leadership role by listening to the client, even if you think you've understood their position, and think things through carefully, taking advice from the partners if necessary before responding to the client.

There is nothing wrong with advising the client that you don't immediately have an answer for them but will investigate and return and report within an agreed timescale.

This will increase rather than decrease the client's respect for you and help you to understand that we never stop learning in this firm.

You've come a long way Michael and we have high hopes for you, don't take your foot off the pedal now.

Passport to Partnership research specifics

The *Passport to Partnership* study collated a number of responses in a conversational style. Two brief but succinct examples which really stood out on the realities of how a firm assesses an individual's 'competence' to lead are showcased below.

- *They need to explain technical data to me in a way that I know they understand it.*
- *What kind of lifestyle does this person have outside of work? We'll be looking at Facebook, Twitter and Google to find out.*

So, if you are going to be considered for leadership and/or partnership in this firm in the future, where do you need to improve your competence?

- In the quality of work presented for review?
- In the way you treat others in the firm?
- In the way you act under pressure?
- In the way you deal with clients?
- In the way you represent the firm publicly?

Partnership pointers

Ask yourself and answer these questions when considering your 'competence' as a leader.

1. What were the greatest challenges that the partners of my firm faced in their careers and how did they handle it?

2. What are the three main traits that my partners are looking for in a leader of our firm?

3. If a Partner saw all my online activity, would their opinion of my suitability for leadership be altered, either way?

CONCLUSION ON
COMPETENCE

What started off in the study as merely a technical 'ante' to get in the game for anyone wishing to be considered as a future partner of their firm has expanded in both definition and scope.

Competence then is the overall outlook of an individual's skill set, behaviors, attitudes and track record during their time with the firm and how that measures up to who the partners want to pass the torch to, when the time comes.

Do you fit the bill?

CHECKLIST

COMPETENCE

Does my work demonstrate a high level of technical ability?

- ☐ 1 Clear strength: "One of the things I do best"
- ☐ 2 Hidden strength: "Others rate me higher than I do"
- ☐ 3 Blind spot: "I rate myself higher than others do"
- ☐ 4 Weakness: "I don't do this well"
- ☐ 5 Untested area: "I don't know enough to answer this question"
- ☐ 6 Don't know: "I need more feedback"

Do I share my knowledge and experience with other members of my team?

- ☐ 1 Clear strength: "One of the things I do best"
- ☐ 2 Hidden strength: "Others rate me higher than I do"
- ☐ 3 Blind spot: "I rate myself higher than others do"
- ☐ 4 Weakness: "I don't do this well"
- ☐ 5 Untested area: "I don't know enough to answer this question"
- ☐ 6 Don't know: "I need more feedback"

Does my competence stretch to managing people?

- ☐ 1 Clear strength: "One of the things I do best"
- ☐ 2 Hidden strength: "Others rate me higher than I do"
- ☐ 3 Blind spot: "I rate myself higher than others do"
- ☐ 4 Weakness: "I don't do this well"
- ☐ 5 Untested area: "I don't know enough to answer this question"
- ☐ 6 Don't know: "I need more feedback"

Do I understand all the ares that the Partners want me to demonstrate my competence in?

- ☐ 1 Clear strength: "One of the things I do best"
- ☐ 2 Hidden strength: "Others rate me higher than I do"
- ☐ 3 Blind spot: "I rate myself higher than others do"
- ☐ 4 Weakness: "I don't do this well"
- ☐ 5 Untested area: "I don't know enough to answer this question"
- ☐ 6 Don't know: "I need more feedback"

Have I got a wide breadth of competence in a range of disciplines performed by my firm?

- ☐ 1 Clear strength: "One of the things I do best"
- ☐ 2 Hidden strength: "Others rate me higher than I do"
- ☐ 3 Blind spot: "I rate myself higher than others do"
- ☐ 4 Weakness: "I don't do this well"
- ☐ 5 Untested area: "I don't know enough to answer this question"
- ☐ 6 Don't know: "I need more feedback"

Perfecting the personal brand

What are the major characteristics that your colleagues would use to describe you if put on the spot?

What are the major characteristics that your Partners would use to describe you if put on the spot?

Is there any discrepancy between the two? What do you need to correct, if anything?

What are the main examples of your command of the 1st C (Competence) that your Partners have seen you demonstrate in your roles in the firm?

Overview

Cultural issues are dynamic, very broad and unique in each firm. As such it is a challenge to summarise them accurately and comprehensively. From the research, however, the wise choice for anyone wishing to get their passport to partnership appears to be to study their firm's existing culture, that of its senior individuals and that of those who have the ear of those senior individuals to understand not only the route to partnership, but the terrain that they need to cross too.

Do any of these scenarios remind you of similar situations in your firm?

The Senior Partner's PA always parks in a certain space even though it has no name nor reserved sign on it and it happens to be one of the closest to the main entrance to the building.

During Christmas parties, the audit department is always required to perform on the karaoke.

Whatever price I calculate a client engagement to be worth, the partner I report to discounts it by 25% right away because 'the client will never pay the fee you came up with.'

You're not alone, it's quite common for each firm to have its individual quirks and idiosyncrasies as a lasting legacy of those who have had the most power within the firm in years gone by.

Yet, however our firm is run, there will come a time when all of this is over. Your ideas on culture will increasingly gain power as you grow in stature within the firm's hierarchy. So thought needs to turn now to studying 'why' the existing culture within the firm and towards clients is as it is, what would happen and who it would upset to change it; and what diplomatic steps can be taken to start the process of change incrementally for the better right now.

How do we do that?

Here are some initial considerations to keep in mind when making sure that the firm's people believe in themselves AND the culture of the organization:

Do not be afraid of what you do not know

You may not be in the corridors of power yet in your firm, but those who are also were not there once. How did they get there and what was the culture of the practice like back then, let's ask them. What do we have to lose?

> The critical first step in establishing a sound professional culture is to make correct judgements on which responsibilities lie at the feet of the organization and which lie at the feet of the individual.

Unify the outlook of the team

The great leader is an ambassador, diplomat and mediator. Every firm has people issues. The skill is in successful reconciliation wherever possible.

Become selfless

The great leaders serve first, without looking for reciprocation. Those you assist are unlikely to forget your kindness when it matters.

Manage expectations

Those you grew up with may well find that you are their boss one day. How well do you know them and how can you manage their reactions and expectations towards their relationship with you when that happens?

When change happens, not everyone adapts in tandem, some never adapt at all

Be prepared to keep yours and the firm's development 'top of mind' at all times as some changes within the firm can be unexpected AND swift. Adaptability without being thrown off course is another key cultural leadership trait. In other words, can the firm depend on you no matter what?

The expert council

Here's what a number of experts exclusively interviewed for this project had to say about CPA firm culture.

Looking back to the beginning of your career, what do you know now about firm culture that you wish you'd known back then?

In truth, when I started at Grant Thornton I had no idea what I wanted to do, other than a deep interest in the business world and wanting to change or create something! That insatiable curiosity in the business world led me to taking on a variety of roles, and ultimately establishing my own business.

Thinking about what I know now, to be honest I knew absolutely nothing when I started my career! Perhaps the most important thing I've learned is that everybody is different – you cannot expect everybody to think like you do (and you are not always right!) and you need to find ways to work with and get the best out of people. Emotional Intelligence is one of the most critical skills, although it's not that common! That is why I always start new business relationships seeking to understand entrepreneurs, what they want to achieve, what gets them excited, and what puts them off. Get to know the people first, then the business.

David Grundy
Grant Thornton

There was no way I could have predicted the exact course my career has taken. And I am thrilled and humbled by what has happened to me. As for the most important thing I have learned, that is simple… follow your heart, do what makes you happy, and make the brave decisions.

Steve Pipe
Ex-KPMG now
Founder of Accountants Changing The World

—

Perhaps the most important thing I've learned is that everybody is different – you cannot expect everybody to think like you do (and you are not always right!) and you need to find ways to work with and get the best out of people.

They become 'leaders' in the profession because they're great at the 'internal' stuff. So the idea of 'leadership' in the sense of powerfully articulating WHY, for example, has never even occurred to them. And equally, they began their careers when you could get by without being pro-active. So inspiring leadership and pro-activity are simply not skillsets they normally possess or know how to sharpen, but they need to.

Paul Dunn
B1G1

Case study on Culture

Deborah had done well. She was bridging the firm's culture gap and fulfilling its desire to be seen as an equal opportunities employer by becoming the practice's standout rising star.

Deborah had long felt marginalized by what she viewed as a chauvinistic fabric to the way the firm did business and promoted people. She had seemed invisible at times through the years.

Her male counterparts had taken advantage of this way of business from time to time and got themselves invited to major client events, sporting hospitality and other 'perks' whilst Deborah had never received so much as an invite. Now, thanks to tremendous technical work and management abilities, she had seen herself rise to the top of the pile and break the 'old boys network' stronghold. A normally placid character, Deborah couldn't help herself in the canteen one lunchtime, in cutting down one of her male colleagues in conversation and flaunting her technical superiority, exposing his relative incomplete knowledge on a tax matter. The issue was reported and like Michael before her (from our case study in the 1st C - Competence), Deborah found herself facing the managing partner.

—

If your contemporaries find cause to mock you, be reassured in the knowledge that your career is going in one direction by your measured behaviours whilst theirs is going in entirely another direction because of their behaviours.

The Managing Partner told her:

As a team we must be conscious of how we make other people feel by our words and actions because we are a team and no-one member is ever greater than that, including myself.

This is a critical stage of your development and as such, you must be very careful to think before you speak and act.

A pause by a senior member of this firm in the face of intense debate or discussion does not indicate mental inferiority but rather that, as a professional they are carefully considering facts, experience, and alternatives open to them, before responding.

If your contemporaries find cause to mock you for that, be reassured in the knowledge that your career is going in one direction by your measured behaviors whilst theirs is going in entirely another direction because of their behaviors.

You've come a long way Deborah and we have high hopes for you, don't slow down now.

Passport to Partnership research specifics

The *Passport to Partnership* study collated a number of responses from existing partners of accounting practices in a conversational style. Examples which really stood out on the realities of individual variances in firm culture are showcased below.

If we really like them, we'll take them out to dinner with the partners to see how they cope in that environment.

Meaning, can they hold their own intellectually in more senior circles? How would they then behave when meeting with other senior executives as a contemporary of theirs? This is a huge consideration for existing partners as the reputation, goodwill and future new business of the practice is influenced greatly by how well the firm is represented by its chosen ambassador (e.g. YOU).

—

The reputation, goodwill and future new business of the practice is at stake in every client encounter.

We like to see if they think that this job is about numbers or about people.

This is self-explanatory but shows the would-be partner where their focus needs to be to make it in the boardroom

Our partners have articulate minds and that's what we want demonstrated by any new appointees.

By 'articulate minds' I discovered that they meant, well read, empathetic, hungry for self-improvement, concise, considered and mature. When evaluating your social behaviors online and offline outside of work, is that how your friends would describe you? If not, what makes you think that this is how the partners, who will decide your future in the firm, will see you?

Partnership pointers

Ask yourself and answer these questions when considering the current and future 'Culture' of your firm.

1. Partner disagreements must have happened in the past at my firm. Without naming names, what did the Managing Partner do about it? Could I handle things that way myself?
2. What do the partners see as culturally critical to the identity of the firm?
3. If I spend all my time rallying against perceived injustices in the way my firm is run, I'm going to be viewed as small fry forever. One way in which I can overcome that sense of injustice is…..

—

By 'articulate minds' I discovered that they meant, well read, empathetic, hungry for self-improvement, concise, considered and mature.

CONCLUSION ON
CULTURE

This second C is a stormy and choppy one, often fraught with political icebergs but navigated diplomatically and with maturity, will lead you through to your third 'C'.

CHECKLIST

CULTURE

Do I earn the respect of the partners in my firm?

- ☐ 1 Clear strength: "One of the things I do best"
- ☐ 2 Hidden strength: "Others rate me higher than I do"
- ☐ 3 Blind spot: "I rate myself higher than others do"
- ☐ 4 Weakness: "I don't do this well"
- ☐ 5 Untested area: "I don't know enough to answer this question"
- ☐ 6 Don't know: "I need more feedback"

Do I earn the respect of my colleagues in the firm?

- ☐ 1 Clear strength: "One of the things I do best"
- ☐ 2 Hidden strength: "Others rate me higher than I do"
- ☐ 3 Blind spot: "I rate myself higher than others do"
- ☐ 4 Weakness: "I don't do this well"
- ☐ 5 Untested area: "I don't know enough to answer this question"
- ☐ 6 Don't know: "I need more feedback"

Can I identify who to ask to obtain ongoing confidential feedback on the above?

- ☐ 1 Clear strength: "One of the things I do best"
- ☐ 2 Hidden strength: "Others rate me higher than I do"
- ☐ 3 Blind spot: "I rate myself higher than others do"
- ☐ 4 Weakness: "I don't do this well"
- ☐ 5 Untested area: "I don't know enough to answer this question"
- ☐ 6 Don't know: "I need more feedback"

How well do I observe the unwritten rules of this firm?

- ☐ 1 Clear strength: "One of the things I do best"
- ☐ 2 Hidden strength: "Others rate me higher than I do"
- ☐ 3 Blind spot: "I rate myself higher than others do"
- ☐ 4 Weakness: "I don't do this well"
- ☐ 5 Untested area: "I don't know enough to answer this question"
- ☐ 6 Don't know: "I need more feedback"

How accomplished am I at not taking sides in matters of office politics?

- ☐ 1 Clear strength: "One of the things I do best"
- ☐ 2 Hidden strength: "Others rate me higher than I do"
- ☐ 3 Blind spot: "I rate myself higher than others do"
- ☐ 4 Weakness: "I don't do this well"
- ☐ 5 Untested area: "I don't know enough to answer this question"
- ☐ 6 Don't know: "I need more feedback"

Cultural identity

What discernments do you already have from your current knowledge of how the promotion system works in your firm that you need to keep in the 'top of mind'?

Cultural blueprint (2nd C)

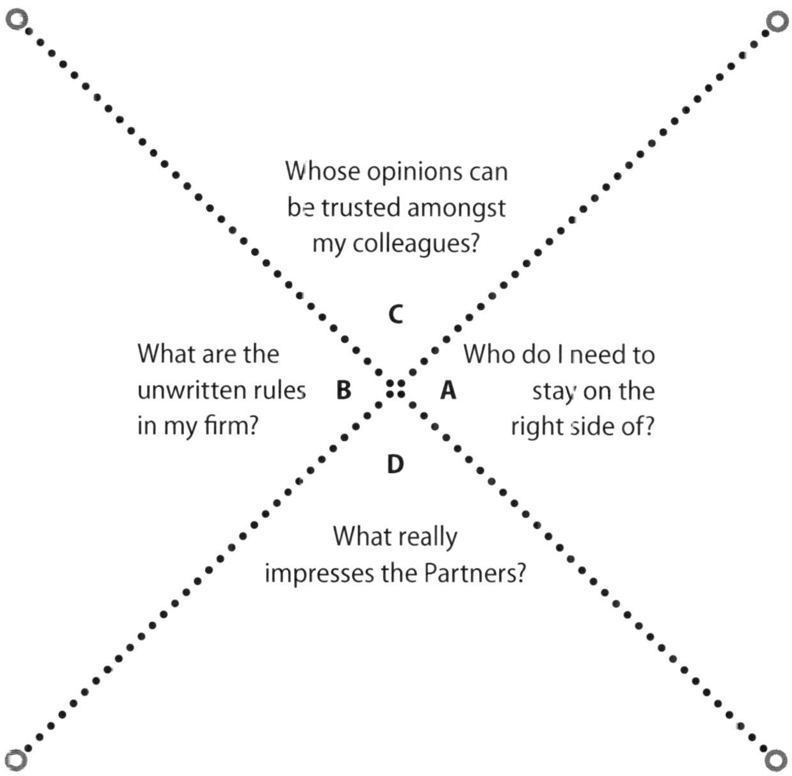

Overview

Ultimately, when we have to interact with clients, subordinates, superiors or peers, the questions are always the same: Who do I need to deliver this information to and what approach would they respond most favorably to?

In arriving at 'Communication' we come to the most intangible of all the components to obtain a 'passport to partnership.

In the research which is on-going and evolving, 'Communication' is the term given in the study to where Partners look for senior managers to demonstrate that they can do two things with existing client relationships:

1. Increase loyalty to the firm through client service and demonstrated empathy.
2. Increase fees through a greater understanding of the client's business and related challenges/needs.

As we've seen with previous 'C' headings, they are common sense and most with a management position within an accounting firm would be able to guess them correctly; but with 'Communication' we have another example of where common sense doesn't seem to widely translate into common application.

Why is that?

Well, the feedback indicates that the top reasons why senior managers, who have access to client relationships, struggle to achieve the two criteria above are:

1. A fear of upsetting the client.
2. A fear of providing poor advice.
3. A lack of business development know-how.
4. A belief that it is not their place to get involved in anything beyond the technical aspects of the engagement.

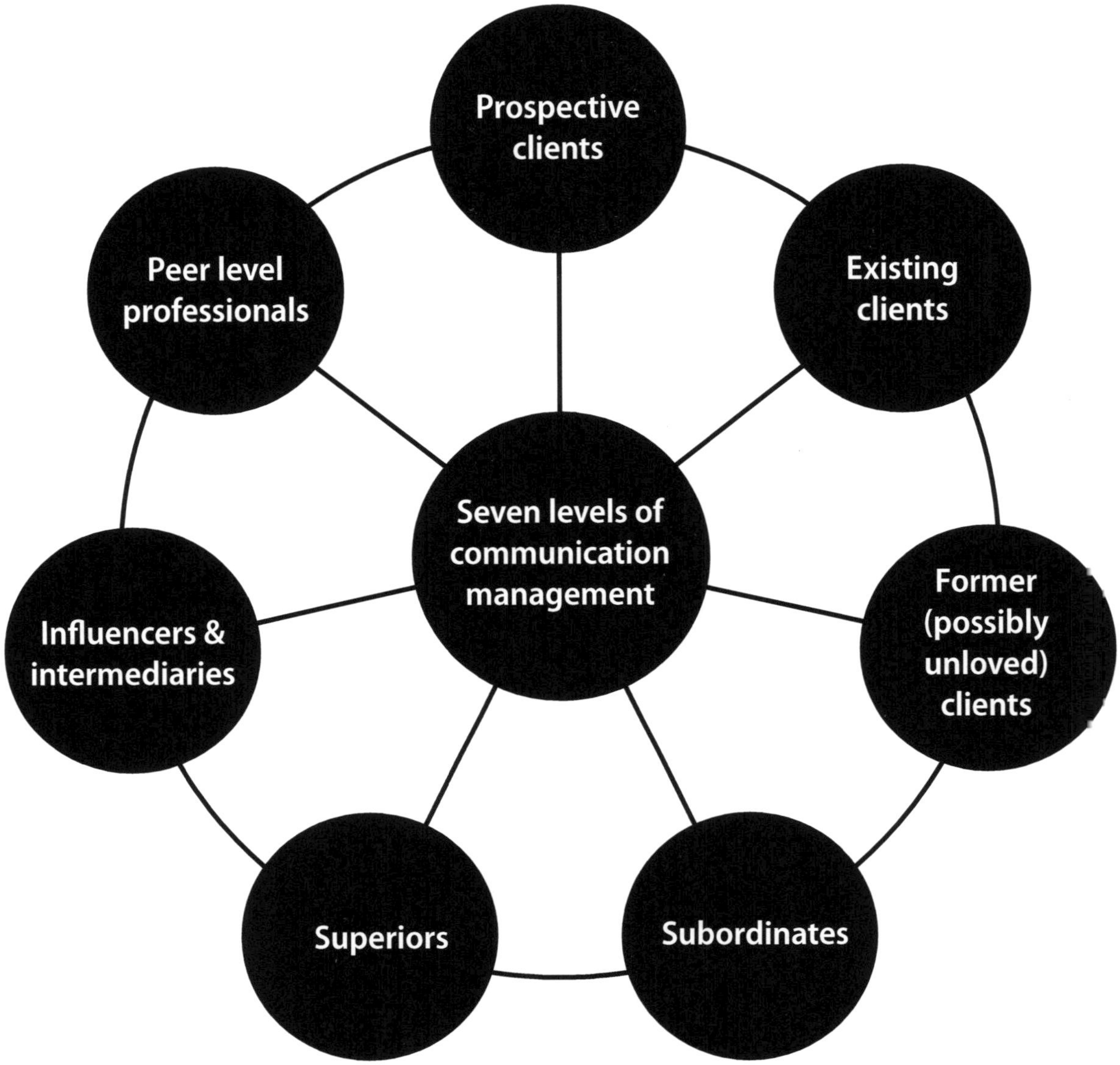
Prospective clients
Existing clients
Former (possibly unloved) clients
Subordinates
Superiors
Influencers & intermediaries
Peer level professionals
Seven levels of communication management

It is illuminating that the same partners who look for the demonstration of these skills from managers also have managers in their firms who fear doing so. Does this provide the firm with a training opportunity or a leadership opportunity; or both?

It would be unfortunate and ironic if a lack of communication internally between partners and managers led to a lack of communication externally with clients and managers.

These are of course general findings however and each firm's culture will set a different precedent.

> The same two traits partners seek most in seniors are the same two traits that stifle growth.

The true take-away from this third 'C' is to underline for senior managers and would-be partners what it can actually take to realize their career goals.

Overcoming the fear of making a mistake and implementing simple relationship building skills can accelerate a manager's push to join the firm's elite.

I've had the benefit of meeting, speaking and observing hundreds of very successful and unsuccessful partners over the last two decades and there is indeed a set of differentiating factors that set a partner apart from the chasing pack. Here are the "best selling behaviors" that I've observed:

Road-tested

None of us can have a track record of partner level excellence on day one in the position but we can be road tested in handling client affairs with integrity, in the pro-active identification of commercial opportunities for a client, in the effective and successful handling of client crises; and a broad range of experience across multiple sectors.

Clients can hear, feel and detect knowledge, assurance and experience. The more real-life understanding we have that demonstrates this, the more we can communicate with the client on their level.

Emotional investment

Sadly, not all partners care about their clients. Not all partners are motivated by a keen sense of wanting to support and assist their clients. Not all partners can relate to, empathize with and think as their clients do. If you can, you'll stand out. That is easy to explain but difficult to consistently implement.

> Too many elements of work for a client are left to chance.

Sense of self-worth

Clients doubt the accountant who talks about incredible service on the website but discounts their bill on the first challenge from them. That doesn't speak of self-worth, it doesn't stick up for the work of the team that reports to the partner and it sets a dangerous precedent with the client going forward. It's a sign of an insufficient understanding of one's own value to the client's business. To be assured is not to be arrogant or cocky but simply 'proven'. Clients will always pay a premium for 'proven'.

Joint accountabilities

A person rarely blames themselves in a conflict and often blames another party, it's just human nature. Through a lack of effective communication and the sense of self-worth described above, I've noticed that many elements of work carried out for a client are often left to chance.

For example, the accounting firm is often blamed when a client incurs a penalty because the client is guilty of not providing true, accurate and on-time information to the accountant. This has happened because the client did not fully understand the dangers of doing so. They are immersed in the affairs of their business. Often, they do not have a comprehension of the various financial reporting requirements on them. Often, they are not educated by their accountant either and it's at times like this that 'assumed knowledge' takes over on both sides.

The accountant has assumed the client would do what was required of them and the client has assumed you'd wave your magic wand and make it all alright if they didn't.

Blame only travels in one direction in such circumstances and the onus, sadly, is on the accountant, whom is the 'expert' here remember, to correctly educate and prompt the client to do their part WITHOUT taking the blame when they do not.

—

Beware the dangers of 'assumed knowledge.'

Here's what a number of experts exclusively interviewed for this project had to say about communication in CPA firms.

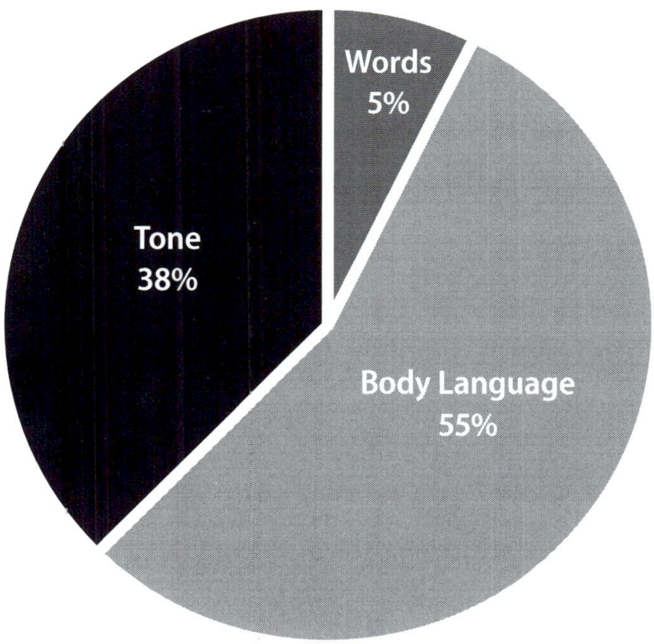

Component parts of how the other person perceives your in-person communication

The expert council

What would be your advice to senior managers wanting to develop their communication abilities?

Technology will change the picture as it has been doing for some time. For example, many believe that in the future we will be able to run our businesses from our mobile devices.

Remember, much of what used to feature in the role of an accountant doesn't now. For example, I spent most of my early career reading over between two sets of Wordperfect accounts and carrying the comptometer machines around – all of which is anathema to today's profession.

So we need to make sure that we spend our time providing what computers will never be able to provide – the trusted relationship to clients and colleagues alike. We need to keep the promises we make and keep them brilliantly.

Steve Pipe
Founder of The Added Value Network

Your people are your biggest asset in an accounting firm. Firms that are investing in their people and spending the time to train and develop them in non-technical areas, like marketing and sales, management and leadership, are going to far surpass firms that can't address this. They will not only grow, but be able to remain independent.

Sarah Johnson Dobek
Inovautus Consulting

Although most firms won't admit it, communication can be an issue internally because partners consciously and actively keep what it takes to join their ranks as a bit of a secret. This can be from a sense of self-preservation (some partners feel challenged, or even threatened, by up-and-coming managers) but mainly because the enthusiasm and drive that you need to find out what is needed to become a partner is much the same as what you need to be successful as a partner, so it's a self-proving "test."

David Grundy
Fundingstore.com

Case study on Communication

Deborah had done well. She was well liked by her clients and colleagues alike. The natural and authentic approach that she had with them had resonated well. The confidence which all stakeholders had in her technical abilities was now being augmented by their level of comfort in her interpersonal skills.

All was going well until she had a new hire join her team. The young man, though talented, did not respond well to her style, was confrontational and even went above her head to the managing partner to express his chauvinistic unwillingness to take direction from a superior of 'the opposite sex'. Whilst the young man was rightly chastised for his behaviour, it didn't change in the short term. Deborah became part incredulous and part indignant. She started choosing other members of her team to give work to and started deliberately selecting this young man for menial tasks well below his ability.

What had started as a minor irritant quickly escalated into a full blown stand off and the threat of a 'silo' micro-culture in her department was becoming a fast reality.

Deborah was out of her depth for the first time in a long time. Her own work suffered as she tried to understand how to manage this situation and find a form of communication that might work with her young miscreant.

The Managing Partner called Deborah into his office. He advised her:

This young man is out of order and make no mistake, if he carries on this way, he will be looking for another position soon enough. You need to know that you have our full backing. However, you also need to know that he comes from a whole family of CPAs including his father and his grandfather. It was a male dominated profession in their time and he has grown up and been educated with that worldview. He now needs educating out of it.

If nothing else, he's got ability and you could sorely use that in your department right now. May I respectfully suggest that you take time out with him away from these premises, in an informal setting. Don't drop down to his level but demonstrate how you've gotten to where you are on merit and that you hold the keys to his future in this firm. Take an interest in him, ask him to collaborate with you on finding a productive way to work together and let me know how it goes.

Your responsibility, Deborah, is to rise above this type of issue. You have an increasingly large responsibility for a major profit center of this firm. When issues like this arise, either manage the person up or manage them out.

Passport to Partnership research specifics

The *Passport to Partnership* study collated a number of responses in a conversational style. Examples which really stood out as the first steps in effective communication are showcased below.

Would we put this person in front of a client?

Meaning: The clients are our source of income, we don't jeopardise that for anything. If we think that this person will do anything less than consolidate the perception of the firm and its people in the eyes of the client, we'll keep them back in the office.

How does this person deal with those in support roles?

Meaning: Let's never forget where we came from or labor under the misguided belief that because someone has less authority in the firm or a lower pay grade, that they are somehow inferior to you.

Partnership pointers

Ask yourself and answer these questions when considering the current and future 'Communication' tactics that you'll employ.

1. If I was my client, boss, peer or subordinate, how would I want to be communicated with by me?
2. What areas of my firm's communication can I improve quickly?
3. I need to understand that it does not matter how I think I'm coming across. I need to understand how the person I'm communicating with thinks I'm coming across.

CONCLUSION ON COMMUNICATION

An advisor is trusted when they can show that they took responsibility for their end of the bargain in the client engagement, educated the client of their responsibilities, offered prompting and assistance throughout but then allowed the client to ultimately govern themselves in terms of following through on their commitments.

This then empowers the advisor to make a commercial decision when the client now faces the consequences, as to whether they want to communicate even more assistance to make things all better for the clients and gain huge appreciation and emotional capital (which can be leveraged for higher fees and referrals in the future but that's a different 'C').

We all know that in the mind of our client, their communication with us forms their perception and their perception becomes the reality.

CHECKLIST

COMMUNICATION

How well do I communicate vital information on time to the Partners?

- ☐ 1 Clear strength: "One of the things I do best"
- ☐ 2 Hidden strength: "Others rate me higher than I do"
- ☐ 3 Blind spot: "I rate myself higher than others do"
- ☐ 4 Weakness: "I don't do this well"
- ☐ 5 Untested area: "I don't know enough to answer this question"
- ☐ 6 Don't know: "I need more feedback"

How well do I communicate to clients the work I'm doing for them and its impact?

- ☐ 1 Clear strength: "One of the things I do best"
- ☐ 2 Hidden strength: "Others rate me higher than I do"
- ☐ 3 Blind spot: "I rate myself higher than others do"
- ☐ 4 Weakness: "I don't do this well"
- ☐ 5 Untested area: "I don't know enough to answer this question"
- ☐ 6 Don't know: "I need more feedback"

How well do I communicate what I require and why to my team?

- ☐ 1 Clear strength: "One of the things I do best"
- ☐ 2 Hidden strength: "Others rate me higher than I do"
- ☐ 3 Blind spot: "I rate myself higher than others do"
- ☐ 4 Weakness: "I don't do this well"
- ☐ 5 Untested area: "I don't know enough to answer this question"
- ☐ 6 Don't know: "I need more feedback"

How well do I build relationships with external influencers?

- ☐ 1 Clear strength: "One of the things I do best"
- ☐ 2 Hidden strength: "Others rate me higher than I do"
- ☐ 3 Blind spot: "I rate myself higher than others do"
- ☐ 4 Weakness: "I don't do this well"
- ☐ 5 Untested area: "I don't know enough to answer this question"
- ☐ 6 Don't know: "I need more feedback"

If I was asked by a potential client today "Why should I join your firm?" how well can I communicate the value we can deliver for our clients at this practice?

- ☐ 1 Clear strength: "One of the things I do best"
- ☐ 2 Hidden strength: "Others rate me higher than I do"
- ☐ 3 Blind spot: "I rate myself higher than others do"
- ☐ 4 Weakness: "I don't do this well"
- ☐ 5 Untested area: "I don't know enough to answer this question"
- ☐ 6 Don't know: "I need more feedback"

My worth

Directions for defining your worth

1. Review your firm's ambitions, ethos, challenges and service line gaps.
2. Based on these, identify the value you bring to your firm and its clients.
3. Rate each area of value from 1(low) to 5 (high) for the outcomes delivered to the client/your firm, how exclusive this area is to you, and the strength of the proof you have for it.

Components of my worth to the firm

COMPONENTS	OUTCOMES	UNIQUENESS	EVIDENCE
e.g. tax expertise	*Savings*	*4*	*Case Studies*

Why am I valuable?

Directions

1. Based on your selected components, prove your value in a sentence.
2. Create a 1-3 sentence summary.
3. Create 3-5 bullet points to expand and add evidence to the summary.
4. Run them by a trusted colleague until the consensus is that they are well honed.

My value in a sentence:

My value in overview format:

My evidence:

External communication social media profiles

Professional headline

Based on the My Value section

What type of clients do you work with?

What outcomes do they get from working with you?

What's a simple statement of why they choose you over the competition?

Summary

Reiterate who you work with and how you help them.

Expand on the outcomes they see in working with you – provide evidence.

Provide evidence that you can do what you say you can.
(Examples of client results, testimonials, case studies, awards, etc.)

Give them a reason to get in touch with you.
(Examples of free report, consultation, seminar invite etc)

Overview

Like it or not, the 21st century accountant is in the relationship building business. When a qualified accountant learns the art of developing those relationships in such a way as they empower the practice to be able to forecast it's new fee income each year, the accountant becomes a profit centre and their value to the firm increases tenfold.

Our fourth 'C' has flirted with being the top answer from respondents in the *Passport to Partnership* study and has featured in over 80% of all firms interviewed as to what makes a senior manager stand out as a potential partner. It will come as no surprise then that the on-going mastery of this discipline of pro-actively winning referred and non-referred new fees should be right up there with developing technical skills, in a senior manager's personal development priorities.

Because 'Selling' (the real name for business development) is still carrying somewhat of a stigma from the cultural traditions of the profession, it is typical to find a manager in a firm who has spent 3-5 years training to obtain their qualifications, a career's worth of experience honing their technical skills and yet less than 12 hours in their entire career working on how to pro-actively win new work. If I were to spend 12 hours with you and benefit from all your experience and technical know-how, realistically, how capable an accountant would I be at the end of it?

That's what I thought.

It could be argued that this skill gap is a direct consequence of what happens when entire generations have been able to build their firms on referral/recurring work alone. What chance then, has a senior manager whose role will be heavily weighted towards the business development tasks that await a 21st century partner, in feeling confident about their abilities to perform in that aspect of partnership? Who will they learn from?

This concern was the second highest in the feedback that came from the Partner hopefuls, who felt their lack of knowledge in how to win new work from non-referred sources, would harm both their chances of obtaining their 'passport' and their ability to 'go places' as a result.

When many existing Partners surveyed look to their pipeline of prospective partners, they see famine rather than feast but yet carry out no internal marketing 'Irrigation' in order to ripen their potential harvest. In turn, managers are often told that in order to make partner, they need to introduce anywhere from $50,000+ of new fees and managers have expressed bewilderment as to how to go about achieving that.

As technology and outsourcing abroad continually erode the compliance foundations of a traditional practice (Wal-Mart tax returns anyone?) the increasing value to our clients will be our advisory services. We've seen and will continue to see firms amplify this element of their service but as everyone starts to amplify their advisory expertise, how will we get heard?

It will become the same scenario as choosing on compliance services alone is now, namely…

1. How much do they cost?
2. Are they local?
3. Do I like them?

As advisory services become the norm in terms of the value that an accounting practice offers, how will we differentiate? The answer is in our ability to sell professionally. How much of a need therefore does our next generation of partners have to develop the skills that their training, to date, has yet to cover?

Let's get some CPE (Control of Prospect's Expectations)

How much chargeable time, if it were to be calculated, is spent on the phone trying to chase up a previous meeting, trying to get an initial meeting, on letters and emails, on writing proposal documents that aren't actually wanted and so on?

—

Smart business development eliminates wasted time and effort.

For the sake of argument, let's say you see 20 new non-referred (you should be converting nearly all of those that are referred) prospects in a calendar year. Let's say that we'd like to have another meeting with 10 of those. Let's say that we spend an hour on writing, calling and emailing them each one before we give up when we get no response. What is your charge out rate per hour? $250? $300? More?

So $250 x 10 prospects is a low-end first year's fee wasted and we all know that my very basic calculation omits many other associated costs. The real investment is in acquiring this work is much higher.

Prospective clients are businesses like any other, having to make decisions each day like any other. Why should the decision whether to meet with you again/employ your firm or not be any different? Why should we have to chase and wait for a response indefinitely, not knowing whether we are pestering them or not?

It is possible and is proven in firms worldwide that we can obtain decisions from clients regarding additional services, prospective clients regarding engaging us and so on, without prolonged wild goose chases.

Which business development metrics should I measure?

Whilst not all of these may be relevant and applicable, in your department or personally, how many of the following have you had this month/year?

- New clients acquired this year that have both said yes and completed the requisite paperwork.
- Prospective clients with whom you have a date set in the diary to receive their decision on whether to come on board with you.
- Prospective clients who attend your events and their most recent conversations with you.
- New business appointments that you've attended this month/year.
- Other appointments you've attended that could progress into fees being realised.
- Prospective clients who didn't reach a decision in years gone by and their progress towards becoming a client.
- Referrals asked for, received and contacted.
- Businesses identified as being desirable clients.
- Conversations held with ex-clients who moved from you because they thought the grass was greener, who might be open to discussing a return to your firm.

If you're doing nothing more than actively measuring the above, you're ahead of around 85% of your competitors.

What measures do you apply in your firm? Could any of the above provide additional support in achieving the growth goals both you and the firm have?

—

THE MAIN FAUX PAS WHEN TRYING TO WIN NEW FEES

Giving away answers

•

Emailing proposals

•

Chasing by phone

•

Low balling fees

•

Selling services rather than outcomes

•

Not asking for the business

•

Waiting for books and records

What makes a written proposal become accepted by the potential client - every time?

Proposal writing is a micro-science in its own right but here are the proven principles that it takes to get proposals accepted.

1 The proposal must clearly demonstrate that we understand what our prospect's business is going through and that the document is offering 'OUTCOMES' which will solve the problem/realise the ambition of the prospect.

2. The proposal must appeal to the emotional as well as the logical arguments for change to induce the prospect to be inclined to be comfortable in doing exactly that.

3. The proposal must 'validate' the firm so that the prospect believes that we can assist them specifically with their challenges, (3rd party evidence, relevant awards etc.) rather than making generic and empty 'website' promises

4. The proposal must contain a price or level of investment that the prospect believes is commensurate with the value being offered (neither over NOR under-priced, hence the micro-science)

5. The outcomes, not services, being offered must contain enough impact for the price to be worth 'affording' for the client, regardless of fees they might currently pay.

6. The toughest one of all - the proposal must deliver the kind of value that makes the prospect want to become a client - NOW!

This skill can take years to refine into an art to where the proposal can represent us sufficiently in our absence and offering compliance services alone will not be enough with our Grade A or B prospects, hence point number 1.

1. The proposal must clearly demonstrate that we understand what our prospect's business is going through and that the document is offering 'OUTCOMES' which will solve the problem/realise the ambition of the prospect.

2. The proposal must appeal to the emotional as well as the logical arguments for change to induce the prospect to be inclined to be comfortable in doing exactly that.

3. The proposal must 'validate' the firm so that the prospect believes that we can assist them specifically with their challenges, (3rd party evidence, relevant awards etc.) rather than making generic and empty 'website' promises.

4. The proposal must contain a price or level of investment that the prospect believes is commensurate with the value being offered (neither over NOR under-priced, hence the micro-science).

5. The outcomes, not services, being offered must contain enough impact for the price to be worth 'affording' for the client, regardless of fees they might currently pay.

6. The toughest one of all - the proposal must deliver the kind of value that makes the prospect want to become a client - NOW!

The key factor about the 'accountant' is that they occupy, should they wish to, a unique position in the minds of their clients. We know it as 'most trusted advisor'. These are assured and successful people and as such they avoid the following traits:

- The needless discounting and low balling of quotes as if you wouldn't get the engagement if it were priced correctly and so prefer to create a false and detrimental impression of your worth right from the outset.
- Discounting when a new piece of work is required by an existing client. If we're asked to do extra work, the client presumably rates us for the work already done. Reflect that value in the fee.
- Discounting when a client disputes the bill. Did you set realistic expectations at the start? Good, charge full value. What are they going to do, leave? You've sprung the bill on them, no wonder they're annoyed, in which case discount and feel lucky to have kept them. Don't make that mistake again.
- Saying accountants are boring in an ironic self-acknowledgement of the commonly held myth surrounding the profession. You're not boring and by trying to curry favour by employing self-deprecating humour we're just perpetuating the myth. Don't perpetuate it, disprove it.
- Taking six weeks to get back to a potential new client after the initial meeting. The excuse 'we're so busy', doesn't tell the client that our firm is in demand; it tells them that they are likely to receive service as crappy as the one they are getting when they are supposed to be in this 'courting' phase with us.

PLEASE STOP...

Confusing referral introductions and warm sales opportunities as being the same thing with the same conversion rate.

•

Claiming low client attrition rates as a barometer of great service.

- Saying you convert 95% of opportunities once your foot is in the door. You're talking about referrals and we all convert 95% of those. Marketing brings about non-referred opportunities, ones that we have to sweat to get but would've been unlikely to have gotten any other way. 25% of those converted is good going initially.
- Claiming low client attrition rates as a barometer of great service. No-one moves accountants unless they need to and very few know why they need to because they are not educated very well by competing firms. Our clients are perpetually at risk. Minimise the liability with actual good service, as in, what the client values about us rather than what we think is good about us.

Here's what a number of expert's exclusively interviewed for this project had to say about conversion in CPA firms.

WHY IS IT SO DIFFICULT TO SELL?

- Selling is stigmatized
- The profession has never been trained to sell
- There is a huge difference between selling and allowing people to buy
- We rarely give them a reason to buy from us that THEY care about

The expert council

In your opinion, what are the greatest opportunities for growth in accounting firms?

More and more we're seeing things that we only dreamt about coming true and totally changing the game. For example, I've always believed that the customer/ Accountant relationship was always about 'connection'. And in those early computer days I used to talk about the customer bringing you in a floppy disk instead of a shoebox.

So now, thanks to the cloud and the brilliant exploitation of it by firms like Xero, you see that connection is there, 24 hours a day. And that's a total game-changer because it means that we now have to look for opportunities to deepen that connection in other ways — so that means two things: niching — seriously becoming the expert in, for example, flower arranging businesses or dentistry or IT or whatever. Going 1 inch wide yet one mile deep as they say.

And the second thing I think is to focus on lifestyle — the lifestyle your ideal customer seeks to have. And then you develop the services and expertise to help them get it. Oh, interestingly, that's NOT about wealth planning necessarily — customers are, I think, looking for much more than extra wealth in the accepted sense — 2008 and the Global Financial Crisis or turmoil changed our definition of what real success means?

Paul Dunn
Chairman B1G1

Why do you feel today's practice leaders are still struggling to grow their firms pro-actively, in general?

Because growing by merger or acquisition is easier than growing by market penetration. Because they have too often ignored relationships that help keep the firm's practice relevant to the changing and dynamic needs of the economic environment. The antiquated ethical rules limit growth, at least by not allowing outside capital. Obviously, so many firms have little sense of marketing, markets, and client relations, and the role of professional and experienced marketers. Stop thinking "we" and instead, think "you".

Bruce W. Marcus
Professional Services Marketing 3.0

Case study on Conversion

Michael had done well. His profile was rising as he became one of the firm's leading 'rainmakers' due to his natural ability to engage and gain the confidence of business owners and influencers alike.

However, when a particularly high profile prospect came into Michael's pipeline, he was VERY excited. He thought about how, when he won this piece of work (which was surely a formality) everyone was going to sit up and take notice from the partners of his farm through to the partners of every competing firm in town. This was the big one.

He had scheduled a call with the president of the company he was trying to win and when Michael called, the President's assistant picked up. Michael introduced himself with dignity and asked for the President. He should have been put on hold but instead, the assistant put the phone to his chest whilst he whispered 'It's Mike Griffiths from PTP on the line for you.' Michael heard the President whisper in reply 'Oh geez, err, yeah he said he would call. Tell him I'm not in the office and you don't know exactly when I'll be back but you'll take a message.'

Michael was incensed! Absolutely incensed. The effort, chargeable time, building of case studies, research for the proposal and everything that had gone into trying to win this engagement and the President wouldn't even take a pre-scheduled call?

When the assistant passed on what Michael already knew, he couldn't take it and shouted back 'You're not sure when he'll be back? That's strange since he's standing right next to you. I just heard him!!"

What followed was awkward but suffice to say the call ended without any further commitment being scheduled. Michael felt low and lied to, but worse was to come.

The assistant had reported what Michael had said to the President. The President reacted to this lack of respect by quickly composing a strongly worded email to Michael's Managing Partner. Within 60 minutes of the call ending. Michael was summonsed.

The Managing Partner called Michael into his office. He advised him:

—

'What on earth were you thinking?!'

What is wrong with you? This is completely unacceptable for someone who is representing our firm in an ambassadorial or rainmaking role. What on earth were you thinking?

You don't need me to tell you how much damage this could do to our reputation. You've managed to annoy the most influential businessman in town. How dare you!

I'm going to put this down to inexperience and call it a blip. You've given me a lot of damage limitation work to do but it's so completely out of character that I'm going to let it go this time.

Before I do though, understand that you have no God-given right to win new work and it takes a long time to do it well but it's not difficult to lose business and you seem to be hell-bent on achieving just that.

Get out of my office, think about what you did and get your head back in the game!

You've come a long way Michael, but your learning curve is just beginning, not ending.

Passport to Partnership research specifics

The *Passport to Partnership* study collated a number of responses in a conversational style. The main example which really stood out as the major indicator of a need for each future leader to be able to 'convert' new business is showcased below and was repeated many times in various different ways.

Cash will work itself out. If this person wants to be considered for partnership in the future, we look at how are they promoting the firm to potential clients now.

Meaning: If you're trusted enough to represent the firm publicly, what perception are clients and potential clients getting about the firm based on their interactions with you?

—

The road to partner starts anew every day.

Partnership pointers

Ask yourself and answer these questions when considering the current and future 'Conversion' tactics that you'll employ.

1. If I was to start today, could I name 4 businesses that I'd like to reach out to?
2. What is our firm's net fee growth goal this year and what can I do to contribute to it?
3. What do I need to do to be able to handle the tough stuff like negotiation, pricing and handling objections? What start to learning these skills can I make today?

CONCLUSION ON
CONVERSION

Please start understanding, valuing and respecting your own value in the marketplace with clients who could not reach their goals without you. Businesses are in need, sometimes desperate need of your technical expertise and caring approach. Take that to them instead because, speaking as one who is looked after well myself, we love it and we are prepared to pay a premium without ever asking for discounts.

CHECKLIST

CONVERSION

Do I have my own pipeline of potential clients?

- ☐ 1 Clear strength: "One of the things I do best"
- ☐ 2 Hidden strength: "Others rate me higher than I do"
- ☐ 3 Blind spot: "I rate myself higher than others do"
- ☐ 4 Weakness: "I don't do this well"
- ☐ 5 Untested area: "I don't know enough to answer this question"
- ☐ 6 Don't know: "I need more feedback"

Do I have my own Linkedin profile?

- ☐ 1 Clear strength: "One of the things I do best"
- ☐ 2 Hidden strength: "Others rate me higher than I do"
- ☐ 3 Blind spot: "I rate myself higher than others do"
- ☐ 4 Weakness: "I don't do this well"
- ☐ 5 Untested area: "I don't know enough to answer this question"
- ☐ 6 Don't know: "I need more feedback"

Am I connected to introducers of new work?

- ☐ 1 Clear strength: "One of the things I do best"
- ☐ 2 Hidden strength: "Others rate me higher than I do"
- ☐ 3 Blind spot: "I rate myself higher than others do"
- ☐ 4 Weakness: "I don't do this well"
- ☐ 5 Untested area: "I don't know enough to answer this question"
- ☐ 6 Don't know: "I need more feedback"

How good do I think I am in converting non-referred opportunities into fee paying clients?

- ☐ 1 Clear strength: "One of the things I do best"
- ☐ 2 Hidden strength: "Others rate me higher than I do"
- ☐ 3 Blind spot: "I rate myself higher than others do"
- ☐ 4 Weakness: "I don't do this well"
- ☐ 5 Untested area: "I don't know enough to answer this question"
- ☐ 6 Don't know: "I need more feedback"

How good am I at handling objections such as when a client questions our fees?

- ☐ 1 Clear strength: "One of the things I do best"
- ☐ 2 Hidden strength: "Others rate me higher than I do"
- ☐ 3 Blind spot: "I rate myself higher than others do"
- ☐ 4 Weakness: "I don't do this well"
- ☐ 5 Untested area: "I don't know enough to answer this question"
- ☐ 6 Don't know: "I need more feedback"

Building your pipeline

Record the businesses you'd ideally like to work with or believe you can add value to below, for future inclusion in your personal pipeline:

Next list any clients which the firm has lost that you feel you could realistically win back:

List any proposals that you were involved with that the firm didn't win. How many of those prospects found what they were looking for? Enter in your pipeline, any that you can't say for sure are happy with their current arrangements:

Detail any current clients that you believe your firm could add value to according to their needs and the services/ outcomes that could be delivered:

Everyone else

List any other businesses that you know (friends, family etc) that you feel you could serve in a way that is superior to their current arrangements:

What 'Stories of Success' can you employ when reaching out to these businesses?

Allocate a conservative figure for the first year's fees that would be derived from winning the business that you've highlighted. What percentage of this figure would be required to justify the increase you desire in your compensation?

Overview

Rising from Senior Manager to Partner often means being promoted ahead of our peers and contemporaries. It creates a gap in earnings, stature and influence compared to those who just yesterday were our colleagues on a level playing field.

It can also mean that if we are coming into a firm from the outside, we are being promoted over people who have served at that firm for many years and understand the 'Culture' (and C) of the firm, a lot better than we do right now.

We may have to lead these people as the head of a department and if so, they'd better be on our side.

This is where the principle of 'Commitment' is applied.

The Partners interviewed in this study commented that they were looking for 'someone with no sense of ego or self-importance, someone who could relate equally as effectively with a client, a partner or an administrative assistant.'

They wanted someone who other employees could look to with respect as an expert, a role model and someone who had a proven track record that justified their appointment.

'Commitment' does not relate to their relationship with existing or new clients but specifically how they conduct themselves behind closed doors at their firm both now as a senior manager and/or then as a new partner. An increase in maturity is applauded by the partners, an increase in arrogance is not.

One partner I interviewed summarised concisely by saying: "When you are promoted to partner, you think you've reached the pinnacle. The truth is that you're actually only on the lower slopes and the hard work and steepest learning curve is still ahead of you'

Climbing that new slope takes Commitment.

How commitment trumps professionalism

This 'learning curve' spoken of that you'll have to go through on an extended basis in your first years as a partner ensures one thing – you're going to make mistakes. Many of these mistakes will be in demonstrating a lack of professionalism as you come to terms with the level of conduct required at partner level.

These slip ups, as long as they are neither prolonged nor oft-repeated will be forgiven quickly by the partners if you demonstrate a commitment to the firm and to consistently improving. (They made these same errors once too!)

—

Rising from Senior Manager to Partner often means being promoted ahead of our peers and contemporaries.

Here are 13 decisions you can make at any time that ensure you commit to having commitment:

1. Who cares, wins!

If nothing else, demonstrate that the sweat and sacrifice that the ownership of the firm have put in to getting it where it is today is not lost on you. Become a historian with regards to your firm's journey and whether dealing with the partners, your team, your clients or your prospective clients, be authentic; because who cares, wins.

2. Agree to learn and be coached

You may have an incredible skill set, you may have experience, you may have exam scores that are one of a kind but you don't have perfection as a professional which means that you need to make perpetual improvement, like we all do.

There will be those within your firm who can offer insight and expertise that you don't have. Since 'Success' is a journey rather than a destination, we can demonstrate that teachable attitude by learning from anyone who has value to add to our knowledge and experience base of life in a professional service firm.

3. Agree to teamwork

One sobering fact about leadership is that leaders are rarely responsible for their successes of their firm but always accountable for its failures. Your team can offer tremendous value, benefit from that and repay your team by offering credit where it's due.

4. Agreeing to two-way investment

You want the firm to develop you, you want them to pay you, you want them to offer you profit shares, bonuses, incentives, new opportunities and so on.

—

As we develop any knowledge on a specific topic, we go from not knowing what we are talking about to thinking that we do, to eventually actually knowing our subject.

Why should they?

It's unlikely that you represent their only option to progress their firm; they are taking a calculated risk with you. Receiving all of the perks of partnership in exchange for 'doing a good job' just isn't good enough.

The Partners want to know that you'll sweat for this firm, that you won't start looking for something elsewhere when times get tough, that they can entrust client relationships to you that have been built over the course of decades.

They want to know that you'll give everything you've got for the sustained prosperity of this firm day in day out, week in week out, month in month out, year in year out.

How can you demonstrate that level of commitment? What are you going to invest, in emotional and tangible terms, to show that you are worthy of all the time effort and trust that the partners will place in you.

This is a two-way investment.

5. Agreeing to acquire & develop wisdom

As we develop any knowledge on a specific topic, we go from not knowing what we are talking about to thinking that we do, to eventually actually knowing our subject.

That's fine for technical topics but leadership and business direction requires wisdom distilled from your own career, the experiences of those around you and those who have gone before you.

Tapping into this wisdom is an investment which pays rich returns. Your commitment to the firm's cause will also be noted as you go the extra mile to seek it out.

As a future leader of a professional service firm, the potential partner must understand that the firm's funds not only pay the direct costs and overheads that the firm incurs in order to deliver its service but it meets the payroll as well.

6. Living the principle of 'Sacred Funds'

There's that old saying about it being a lot easier to spend someone else's money than our own.

As a future leader of a professional service firm, the potential partner must understand that the firm's funds not only pay the direct costs and overheads that the firm incurs in order to deliver its service but it meets the payroll as well. In other words, those funds pay for mortgages, vehicles, food, and heat of however many people your firm employs at a given time.

Furthermore, these funds are the fruits of the efforts of the existing partners over an extended period. They must be treated with the respect that they deserve and the reverence of what they provide.

If you get given the cheque book, the credit card or some other authorisation to spend the organisation's money, treat it as you would your own….or better.

7. Take your team with you

Your passage to partnership may occur at the expense of or ahead of someone else's. This is a delicate political situation to navigate for the new partner. Therefore, demonstrate to your

Your direct reports
Your partners
Your introducers
Sources of professional relationships to continually build
Your team
Your intermediaries
Your clients

colleagues that nothing has changed and that there is no ego as a result of your pending or confirmed promotion.

Rather, strive in natural ways to increase your service and support of them and their careers, that's what a leader would do.

8. Take your clients with you

Again, this requires little more explanation than is contained in point 7. The fact that you are going to or have been made a partner changes nothing except the increased expectations that those who work with you, are entitled to have of you.

9. Resource as a communal means

If your firm has a booking policy for its meeting rooms, you don't overrule it. If your firm has a policy for the distribution of human resource to work on client matters, you don't circumnavigate the lines of authorisation that exist.

Respect everyone's right to use the same resources as you and resist the temptation to pull rank when you didn't follow the correct protocol.

10. Perpetual relationship building

This goes for your relationships with:

- Your Partners
- Your Team
- Your Clients
- Your Intermediaries
- Your Introducers
- Your Direct Reports

Increasingly, people are going to look to you to set the standard on the quality of relationships that your firm is known for both externally and internally. What are they going to see when they look to you?

11. Expert intolerance

As a partner, time will evaporate as your list of responsibilities and deadlines increases. In the past, your colleagues will have felt no hesitation in entering your office for a chat about the game last night or the movie on TV. They will not appreciate the pressure that you are now under.

You however, need to shut off from everyone at times to ensure that you produce quality work for your firm and your clients. You need to let them know this without them feeling offended. Find a word, a look, a sign or something else that ensures people leave you alone when they need to.

Respect everyone's right to use the same resources as you and resist the temptation to pull rank when you didn't follow the correct protocol.

12. Continual deposits in the goodwill account

There will be many times that you'll require your team to go the extra mile for you, to stay late, to work extra hard, maybe even to correct your mistakes.

Apart from it not requiring a reason to be classed as 'best practice', if nothing else, it is wise to have a team willing to carry out the above tasks for you when required. If they feel a tremendous amount of goodwill towards you, they'll answer the call.

You'll achieve this if your commitment to them is unfailing in between times.

13. Sincere powerful passion

Hopefully this is why you tried so hard to reach the top in the first place. You want to be the expert, you want to help your clients achieve their goals, and you want to assist in the development of the next generation of leaders in your firm.

Whatever the motive, your passion for building the firm will become contagious not just within the members of your team but with the partners and the wider firm as a whole.

You can make the decision to follow the traditions of the profession and fall into line, or commit to being truly committed and take the performance and achievements of your firm onto a whole new level.

The expert council

From your wealth of experience, what is going to be the single biggest challenge for the next generation of practice leaders?

Letting bad habits die. There are many legacy practices and systems in current accounting firms that haven't changed in 20+ years. The next generation will struggle with managing multiple generations at once and their ability (or willingness) to adapt to change.

Damien Greathead
2020 Group USA

It's their adherence to an outdated model. They refuse to look at how they communicate, price and create value. It's just a broken business model. It's not all that different to Napster and how it illustrated the obsolete state of the traditional music industry business model. We need business model innovation to add more value to the customer to begin with. Right now we're working with a hundred year old business model. The world has changed.

Ron Baker
Verasage Institute

Learn to think imaginatively, in terms of your ability to serve clients. Learn to leverage the skills of younger people to your firm's advantage, rather than on the basis of longevity. Concentrate on client service. Your skills should be a given, not a reason to retain you. Ask yourself every day – this is the way we did it yesterday. Is it still the best way today? Thinking this way produces amazing results.

Bruce W. Marcus
Professional Services Marketing 3.0

Passport to Partnership research specifics

The *Passport to Partnership* study collated a number of responses in a conversational style. The need for commitment is showcased below and was repeated many times in various different ways.

So many use us as a stepping stone and we're now trying to determine who those are at the interview stage

Proof if any were needed that long term 'commitment' as not a 'given' in the next generation of accounting professionals.

One question we ask is: Would we want to pass our firm onto someone like this?

At all times, our performance is being evaluated by those in a position to progress our careers.

At all times, our performance is being evaluated by those in a position to progress our careers.

If we're going to pay a reasonable salary, we want to make sure that we're going to see a return in the short and long term

A salary is a calculated investment decision made by equity holders in the firm with a view to providing a return for them on a recurring basis.

Case study on Commitment

Deborah had been the toast of the firm after landing what was widely regarded as being THE major client on the firm's wish list.

Although it had been a team effort, Deborah had led the engagement team, built the relationships, written the proposal and closed the deal. This had provided her with a huge amount of Kudos from colleagues and peers alike.

She was committed to developing the relationship ever further as well as she formed excellent relationships with all key stakeholders in the client's business.

On a call to setup some training for the client, Deborah's contact expressed that they wanted her and not the firm's Managing Partner involved on the session. They cited the Managing Partner's lack of likeability and embarrassingly, personal hygiene, as the reasons behind this.

Deborah, nervous and not having been put in this situation before, quickly agreed with the client, instantly placing her commitment in the wrong place.

In Deborah's firm, all calls were recorded and randomly sampled. She felt she'd taken a calculated risk in not reporting the details of the call to her Managing Partner as the chances of that particular call being selected for the review were almost nil.

Luck was not on her side.

The Managing Partner heard the call and was personally hurt by Deborah's willingness to agree with the client's assessment of him and this was compounded by her lack of disclosure that it had happened after the fact.

The Managing Partner was unwilling to discuss this with her personally this time and simply sent an official letter advising her of her misconduct and the possible future repercussions of any repeat of this behaviour.

Deborah realised that her commitment to the firm is what had gotten her to where she was in the first place and that no matter how big the client, professional distance was always to be maintained in the interests of her keeping the trust of the partners that she was committed to the cause and worthy of further advancement in the firm.

Partnership pointers

Ask yourself and answer these questions when considering the current and future 'Commitment' behaviours that you'll employ.

1. What is my first reaction to being asked to work outside of my normal hours?
2. How well do I understand the history and ethos of this firm and do I appreciate what the current partners have had to do to get this firm to where it can afford to pay me today?
3. Is my focus on my own progression at any cost or are my colleagues and their feelings and futures on my mind at the same time?

CONCLUSION ON
COMMITMENT

There's no doubt that consistent commitment is not an as widely-practiced as current partners of accounting firms might like to think.

Business success is built on a dedicated team with a shared vision giving their all for the realisation of that vision and the development of the next one.

Commitment is at first a resolve arrived at in the mind, secondly a decision made to practice personal integrity and thirdly consistent behaviours which form habits which in turn construct the foundation of your reputation amongst your colleagues.

When you commit to commitment, you stamp your passport to partnership with the major behavioural trait that existing partners in the firm notice.

CHECKLIST

COMMITMENT

Do I work extra hours without being asked?

- ☐ 1 Clear strength: "One of the things I do best"
- ☐ 2 Hidden strength: "Others rate me higher than I do"
- ☐ 3 Blind spot: "I rate myself higher than others do"
- ☐ 4 Weakness: "I don't do this well"
- ☐ 5 Untested area: "I don't know enough to answer this question"
- ☐ 6 Don't know: "I need more feedback"

Do I work extra hours without being paid?

- ☐ 1 Clear strength: "One of the things I do best"
- ☐ 2 Hidden strength: "Others rate me higher than I do"
- ☐ 3 Blind spot: "I rate myself higher than others do"
- ☐ 4 Weakness: "I don't do this well"
- ☐ 5 Untested area: "I don't know enough to answer this question"
- ☐ 6 Don't know: "I need more feedback"

Do I seem committed to the partners in my firm?

- ☐ 1 Clear strength: "One of the things I do best"
- ☐ 2 Hidden strength: "Others rate me higher than I do"
- ☐ 3 Blind spot: "I rate myself higher than others do"
- ☐ 4 Weakness: "I don't do this well"
- ☐ 5 Untested area: "I don't know enough to answer this question"
- ☐ 6 Don't know: "I need more feedback"

When work gets piled on me, do I act maturely in dealing with it?

- ☐ 1 Clear strength: "One of the things I do best"
- ☐ 2 Hidden strength: "Others rate me higher than I do"
- ☐ 3 Blind spot: "I rate myself higher than others do"
- ☐ 4 Weakness: "I don't do this well"
- ☐ 5 Untested area: "I don't know enough to answer this question"
- ☐ 6 Don't know: "I need more feedback"

Do I demonstrate that I'm working for the good of the firm ahead of the good of my career?

- ☐ 1 Clear strength: "One of the things I do best"
- ☐ 2 Hidden strength: "Others rate me higher than I do"
- ☐ 3 Blind spot: "I rate myself higher than others do"
- ☐ 4 Weakness: "I don't do this well"
- ☐ 5 Untested area: "I don't know enough to answer this question"
- ☐ 6 Don't know: "I need more feedback"

Showing your true colors

What kind of loyalty does the firm place a high value on? *For example working extra hours without being asked, informing them on competitor activity, making them aware of job offers you've received and rejected?*

Based on what the Partners place a high value on, what commitment can you actively demonstrate to the firm on an ongoing basis?

Write down your shortlist of people in your team/department you feel that you can instill this same sense of commitment in and how you are going to go about it.

Overview

Now we move onto our sixth 'C' - Challenges

Again the heading has more than a single application, which we'll explore here.

Ultimately, the Partners interviewed in our research broke 'Challenges' down into two key areas:

1. The ability for a manager to pull the firm out of the mire when there's a problem
2. The ability for a manager to pull the client out of the mire when there's a problem

Naturally, because this became a consensus answer, we speculated as to how often an occurrence one of the above would be, for a manager to need to be able to demonstrate their abilities in rescuing a client or the firm as a result of a previously substantial error.

It would appear to be fairly commonplace.

Regardless of the reason though, the partners we spoke to looked to the manager to handle such situations with calmness, decisiveness and integrity.

It is that decisiveness where the majority felt that they weren't seeing this behaviour demonstrated by their managers. The managers, perhaps understandably, looked for confirmation that their course of action was partner-approved.

The partners however, wanted the managers to demonstrate that they could make the bold decisions in preparation for when there were none more senior to ask.

Challenges then, is defined by the attitude, experience, critical problem solving skills and logical process abilities; that a manager can show themselves to be in possession of, when the pressure is on. This is our sixth 'C'.

Get challenged, get excited

It's human nature for us to feel discouraged, inconvenienced or demoralised by anything that gets in the way during the working week of us carrying out that which we'd planned to do. This leads us to viewing a challenge, issue or problem in a negative light.

Viewed differently however, challenges provide our training, test our resolve, improve our resilience and form our leadership skill set.

—

Ultimately, the Partners interviewed in our research broke Challenges down into two key areas:
The ability for a manager to pull the firm out of the mire when there's a problem
The ability for a manager to pull the client out of the mire when there's a problem

What challenges do we encounter on the road to partnership?

1. Health

Our career health can be blighted by lapses in judgment, apathetic outlooks and 'Knowledge neglect'. 'Knowledge neglect' is the stage of your career that you get to where you're either too busy, too disinterested, or both. In continuing to learn and hone your skills as a leader, as soon as we stop wanting to learn about leadership, we should stop trying to lead.

Stress

Stress seems to have become an overused word to describe everything from being very busy through to genuine psychological pain. Stress is a constant companion in running a successful and competitive CPA firm and only the triple combination of the very best in processes, profitability and personnel can elevate this on an ongoing basis. If you're already suffering from stress perform this diagnostic immediately:

1. Have you got the level of competence required for the work you're been asked to carry out? (yes/no)
2. Have you got scheduled breaks in your day where you do not look or work on anything? (yes/no)

3. Do you have at least three evenings a week free from work related activities? (yes/no)
4. Do you diarise meetings and tasks, scheduling at least 15 minutes more than you need for each of them? (yes/no)
5. Do you enjoy the work you're doing and believe in the firm/people you're working for (yes/no)

Address any 'no' you might have scored, immediately.

Political infighting

How often have you encountered the following?

1. An individual working well below their capability?
2. An individual jealous of a co-worker?
3. An individual furious about the amount of work on their desk compared with the amount of money in their pay check?
4. An individual comparing their pay check with one of a colleague who appears to do less than 50% of the work but for the same or better pay?
5. An individual who has parked in an unmarked parking bay which is 'understood' to be someone else's?
6. An individual who has been unsuccessful in applying for a promotion when the job has gone to a family member of the partner who runs the department despite them having no experience and half the skill set?

And so on it goes. Political infighting is career cancer and must be avoided at all costs. That's a lot easier said than done, but it must.

From experience, true colours tend to come out in the end and the ownership of the CPA firm you work in see everybody for who they really are anyway. If they don't, then it's time to question whether you are in the right CPA firm.

Going stale

Most of us have experienced that 'not another year at this firm' feeling when January comes around. The skill is making sure that there are enough challenges to keep our skills sharp and developing whilst staying on the right side of work/life balance.

2. Wealth

Poor customer service

Is another proven method for retarding growth. A $10,000 client is worth $100,000 minimum to your firm before referred work and cross selling are taken into consideration and it could easily cost that same $100,000 just to try and replace that core work from the client alone, before all the add-ons.

The client may not always be right, but they do always pay your salary.

"Challenges" is defined by the attitude, experience, critical problem solving skills and logical process abilities that a manager can show themselves to be in possession of when the pressure is on.

No new business

A reliance on referral work leads to two main concerns:

1. Being unable to forecast the regularity and amount of work which can be billed each year and…
2. The uncontrollable quality of client which a firm commits to working with.

Business development, as we explored in the 4th C is a foundational behaviour of the 21st century CPA and new fees, higher fees, more enjoyable work should always be being targeted by the firm.

Frozen fees

Our bills went up last year. The client's bills went up last year. Yet so many firms think that they somehow can't raise their fees because the client might leave. Then let them, especially if they are unprofitable ones that don't refer profitable work to compensate you.

'But what if we can't replace them?' is the usual response. 'You must not be offering anything more attractive than the worst of your competitors' is a valid reply.

Your best prospective clients are almost always your competitor's clients. If you deliver mutually recognised value to your clients, raise your fees.

3. Stealth

Litigation

Always be aware of the silent spectre of litigation from a client, a competitor, a supplier or some other unexpected source. Litigation can disable a firm's profitability by tying it up in bureaucratic red tape whether justified or no.

Competition

Today, one of your competing firms successfully or unsuccessfully contacted/wrote to/met one of your existing clients. This tactic will only increase as time goes on… because it's successful.

Legislation

Audit levels rise, compliance is increasingly taken care of by technology. The market for the first becomes the preserve of the larger firms and the market for the latter becomes the preserve of the cheapest firms. How will you ensure profitability for your firm in the face of increasingly relaxed legislation that allows these two scenarios to occur?

—

The leaders of our firm in the future are going to have to demonstrate at manager stage that they can rescue both the client and the firm from tough situations. That ability is a key indicator that we have the right person ready to assume control.

The expert council

What is going to be the single biggest challenge for the next generation of practice leaders?

My experience is that it is two things.

Firstly you've got to get the fundamentals right as I said in my earlier answer. There's no point in trying anything clever if you've got giant leaks in your business development pipeline. If you find yourself saying "we get all our business from word of mouth", if you haven't built detailed profiles of your ideal clients, if you don't understand the business triggers that cause them to change suppliers, if you don't have 3 or 4 lead generation strategies you've mastered or you don't have a pre-planned process in place for follow-up then you're probably in trouble.

Once you do have those fundamentals in place then your advantage, by its very nature, must come from something that's unique to you.

Every firm and every individual is different. We all have a unique set of skills and capabilities. By systematically reviewing what it is your ideal clients really value and matching that with your specific capabilities you can almost always find something that sets you apart from your competitors.

And the truth is that most of your competitors aren't really that great at marketing. So even if they could reproduce what you're doing, it's highly likely that they won't.

Ian Brodie
Marketing Strategist

I think I have already alluded to this in my earlier replies. The bottom line is that we are set for more change in the next five years than we have seen in the last 20 years. Those changes will be driven externally compared to the last 50 years when change has largely come about because of "internal" change driven by regulators. I foresee access barriers being removed and geographic boundaries being widened.

What to do? Now isn't the time to bury heads in the sand or procrastinate. NOW is the time for innovative planning and implementation. NOW is the time to advance the quality of client service. NOW, more than ever before firms need to be clear regarding their ROI proposition to clients. Now, is the time to specialise – by industry and by service.

Mark Lloydbottom
Practice Management Strategies

Early adopters for the amazing IT that is driving efficiencies for compliance work would lend itself to increasing market share at low prices for that compliance work. Aggressive acquisitions to compliment this is a massive opportunity

Additionally the insatiable appetite to broaden the range of services building on client loyalty is equally as opportunistic. Right now tax strategies, wealth management and General Insurance opportunities are the winners.

Gordon Gilchrist
2020 Group

Passport to Partnership research specifics

The *Passport to Partnership* study collated a number of responses in a conversational style. The need for professionals who can remain calm in the storm is showcased below and was repeated many times in various different ways.

'The Leaders of our firm in the future are going to have to demonstrate at manager stage that they can rescue both the client and the firm from tough situations. That ability is a key indicator that we have the right person ready to assume control.'

Case study on Challenges

Michael had gotten to the end of a tiring and challenging financial year. He was pleased with the fruits of his labours as he had hit both his billing and profitability targets which had been set for him by his managing partner 12 months earlier.

In preparing for his review of this financial performance with the Managing Partner, his sense of achievement made the challenges that had come his way over the year (including some internal roadblocks that seemed to be trying to prevent his success) seem worthwhile and it was with an air of quiet satisfaction that he entered the managing partner's office.

'Michael…' began the managing partner; 'I and the partners are pleased that you've managed to demonstrate that you are equal to the expectations that we've had of you in terms of your financial performance'. 'However, this year has seen an unprecedented rise in staff salary increases, corporate benefits such as your new car and increased utility, technology and maintenance bills across the entire firm'.

'As one of our rainmakers therefore, we have reviewed your forecasts for the next 12 month period and are disappointed to see a budgeted increase of less than the rate of inflation, which if this is all you achieved, would mean the firm taking a backwards step in terms of your contribution to our revenues over the next year.'

'WHOA, hang on a minute!' exclaimed Michael, practically yelling. 'These figures are the best performance any senior manager has EVER posted in this firm and I dare to say a lot better than some of the other partners too. We're at capacity with the work I've introduced. I asked you for increased staff provision for this next year six months and it was refused, with my instruction being to increase productivity from existing resources. Well, we're at breaking point now and what you're asking is unworkable.'

'Really? At breaking point? Explain to me then why there is no-one from your department moving any faster than a normal walking pace around this building? Why are we allowing extended lunch breaks with no catch up…'

'YOU WON'T AUTHORISE OVERTIME!!'

'…Michael, you're going to get one warning about raising your voice in front of me, before disciplinary action is brought against you.

'As I was saying, there are numerous extended lunch breaks and your team have got time to chat at the water cooler and I've yet to hear a conversation about work topics go on there.

'You need to stop thinking you've made it just because you've hit your numbers for once. You need to understand that every wage rise, every extended lunch break, every perk that we offer is funded out of profitability.

'My job is to manage the cash flow of this firm amongst other things and your job is to wake up, stop patting yourself on the back and revise these forecasts in line with our stated objectives for growth next year as can be found in the strategic plan.

'You've had a good year Michael, and there's a lot of goodwill for you here, but when it comes to the numbers, you're only as good as today's performance. Let's see what you can really do in this firm.'

Partnership pointers

Ask yourself and answer these questions when considering the current and future 'Challenges' behaviours that you'll employ.

1. What is my first reaction to being notified of a client complaint?
2. How well do I understand the role that everyone else plays in the firm, especially the challenges faced by its leadership?
3. Is my focus on making myself look good or solving issues for the firm and its clients as effectively and efficiently as I know how?

CONCLUSION ON CHALLENGES

When challenges come our way, regardless of what shape or form they arrive in, our world seems to lose a bit of brightness, there's a little knot in the gut and a sense of peace broken.

The challenge is of course irrelevant. What is being measured here is our response to the challenges and what would happen if the existing partners of the firm were to entrust us with their livelihoods, their client base, their finances and their commitment to meeting the payroll obligation that they have each month.

The old saying that 'proper planning prevents poor performance' was never more apt than here.

Our resolve, attitude, character, integrity, ethics and competence are examined under the microscope when challenges come calling in our careers.

The question is, if we were watching our own responses to these trials, would we be in favour of appointing ourselves as the next partner of the firm?

CHECKLIST

CHALLENGES

How do I react to issues in my work day?

- ☐ 1 Clear strength: "One of the things I do best"
- ☐ 2 Hidden strength: "Others rate me higher than I do"
- ☐ 3 Blind spot: "I rate myself higher than others do"
- ☐ 4 Weakness: "I don't do this well"
- ☐ 5 Untested area: "I don't know enough to answer this question"
- ☐ 6 Don't know: "I need more feedback"

How fast do I weigh up the situation before speaking or taking action?

- ☐ 1 Clear strength: "One of the things I do best"
- ☐ 2 Hidden strength: "Others rate me higher than I do"
- ☐ 3 Blind spot: "I rate myself higher than others do"
- ☐ 4 Weakness: "I don't do this well"
- ☐ 5 Untested area: "I don't know enough to answer this question"
- ☐ 6 Don't know: "I need more feedback"

How well do I consider other people's opinions as well as my own?

- ☐ 1 Clear strength: "One of the things I do best"
- ☐ 2 Hidden strength: "Others rate me higher than I do"
- ☐ 3 Blind spot: "I rate myself higher than others do"
- ☐ 4 Weakness: "I don't do this well"
- ☐ 5 Untested area: "I don't know enough to answer this question"
- ☐ 6 Don't know: "I need more feedback"

How good is my track record of acting in the client's best interests?

- ☐ 1 Clear strength: "One of the things I do best"
- ☐ 2 Hidden strength: "Others rate me higher than I do"
- ☐ 3 Blind spot: "I rate myself higher than others do"
- ☐ 4 Weakness: "I don't do this well"
- ☐ 5 Untested area: "I don't know enough to answer this question"
- ☐ 6 Don't know: "I need more feedback"

Do I have a strong appetite for problem solving/trouble shooting?

- ☐ 1 Clear strength: "One of the things I do best"
- ☐ 2 Hidden strength: "Others rate me higher than I do"
- ☐ 3 Blind spot: "I rate myself higher than others do"
- ☐ 4 Weakness: "I don't do this well"
- ☐ 5 Untested area: "I don't know enough to answer this question"
- ☐ 6 Don't know: "I need more feedback"

Battles won and lost

What are some examples of challenges that you've overcome for/in the firm?

What are your three biggest failures in your career and what have been the key lessons that you've taken from them?

What Health, Stealth & Wealth Challenges do you foresee in your career? (For example stress, political infighting, legislative changes, fee pressure etc) and what will be your measures to combat them?

CHALLENGE	COMBATIVE ACTION TO TAKE
Health e.g. *Hours worked*	
Stealth e.g. *Competitor Marketing*	
Wealth e.g. *Static fees*	

Overview

We've reached the end of the voyage and so to our 7th and final C – Commercial Awareness.

A big concern in recent years has been how the incoming partners will purchase equity or fund the capital account and exit of a retiring partner. Much has been written that examines the mathematical complexities of this topic but the bottom line is simple. Would-be partners in the age demographic of 28-42 are part of a generation who are already heavily borrowed in the form of credit card debt, mortgage debt and other forms of personal loans.

Their capacity to borrow in the current economy is extremely limited and it would appear that this will be the environment for the foreseeable future. In turn, the bank's willingness to lend has also been largely withdrawn in recent years.

This has produced a cash impasse that has forced Partners to consider gifting equity, especially on the basis of time served in the firm. There is not scope within this piece to give full examination of best practice within this area except to highlight that 72% of partners surveyed highlighted that a Senior Manager's ability to 'buy in' to the firm and assume responsibility for funding the retirement plans of exiting partners; was amongst their top 3 concerns about passing their practice on to existing employees.

Some partners also connected the tenacity to raise funds with the desired level of ambition that they were looking for from those that they were to hand the practice over to in the future.

Those without such ability need not fear however. The cash principle was underpinned by the following disclaimer from several respondents we spoke to, 'Clear and regular displays of talent and ambition from our senior staff whilst salaried, will always trump whether they have cash or not in our deliberations.'

So if the potential partner doesn't have or doesn't need cash to buy equity in the firm, what do they need? They need to understand what a partner goes through.

Have you ever thought about what a day is like in the life of an accounting firm partner?

Imagine coming in earlier than everyone, leaving later than everyone and being paid last.

Imagine having to deal with the personnel disputes, the three who have called in sick when work in progress needs to be freed up, the major client who advises that they are moving to the competition, the lack of new business opportunities being created by marketing, the failure of referral sources to return the favour of introducing work to your firm in the way you have done for them, the major fallout with another partner over his departments productivity and apathetic attitude towards billing, the changes in audit legislation leaving you wondering where the money is coming from over the next few years; and it's not even 9 am yet!

So, when you become a partner and become responsible for handling some or all of these real life and real time issues, will you choose to just do what it takes to survive or to thrive?

Survive or thrive?

Recently at the time of writing, there was a particularly good (and rare) piece of television here in the UK called 'Call The Midwife'.

I hadn't been aware of the series that preceded it and thought it was a one-off. However, in this episode, two nurses discuss a particular case and one mentions that the death certificate of an individual who slaved away in a workhouse their entire career read 'Cause of Death – Failure to Thrive'.

This got me thinking about our practices. Are our firms likely to die this year? I most certainly hope not. In life though, we must progress and grow, that's the point of all this effort after all. So if growth is on our agenda for any given year in terms of fees, clients, number of people employed etc. and we don't achieve what we had planned to, our firm won't have died necessarily, but another year of opportunity will have.

TOP 5 REASONS WHY FIRMS DON'T THRIVE

- We're too busy
- We just don't know how
- People just don't want to change their accountant
- We don't want to upset the client's relationship with us
- We're unsure and don't know where or how to begin

I then thought about all my meetings, numbering into the several thousands, with senior partners, managing partners, partners with particular portfolios, senior managers and practice managers over the years, where they had explained to me why they weren't seeing the growth in the firm and the level of personal progress and remuneration that they'd wanted. I saw patterns emerge over and over again.

Here for you then are the top five reasons (you decide if they are excuses or not) why firms don't thrive and the recommended solutions.

1. We're just too busy

This is one I confess to never having fully understood. It is a reason we'd never use in any other central area of life. If something is critical or vital to us, we make time for it. If we are dog lovers, are we too busy to feed or walk the dog? No, because the dog suffers otherwise, their growth is harmed and we don't want that. If our child is bullied in school, do we find the time the go and see the principal to ensure our child's safety? Of course we do. Our child suffers otherwise, their growth is harmed and we don't want that. So presumably, if we don't want our business to suffer either, we don't harm growth by claiming to be too busy.

What we're actually saying is that for some reason, growth and what it takes to achieve it; is less important than dealing with what we already have on our plates now. If this is true, I'd advise you to stop hurting yourselves by paying lip service to wanting to grow. If it is not true, then I'd recommend a re-evaluation of why we're actually in practice and what would really happen if we allowed some client work which is both time hungry and profitability impoverished, to find a new home and free us up to build something better.

The greatest growth always occurs in the steepest learning curves however and I'm sure when you studied accountancy and sat your exams as a soon to be qualified accountant, the reality of being in practice was still something of a culture shock regardless.

In my experience, if something is important enough to us, there's no such thing as being too busy to attend to it.

2. We just don't know how

Here's one that I completely understand. It is so frustrating to recognise the potential, maybe even see in detail what can be achieved within a business, and then have no idea how to go about making it a reality.

The disciplines and skill set required to grow the firm beyond the rate of referred work that comes in, minus annual attrition, is not always natural. It is a time commitment, it is uncomfortable. It is however, still necessary. There are so many skills that we don't stop learning because the first steps are daunting.

In fact, the greatest growth always occurs in the steepest learning curves. however and I'm sure when you studied accountancy and sat your exams as a soon to be qualified accountant, the reality of being in practice was still something of a culture shock regardless.

If 'we just don't know how' is having a crippling effect in your firm, how about committing to nothing more than 'baby steps' and make sure that progress is achieved little and often to effect great change over the longer term. It's the commitment that's the hard part. Beat that and we're making progress already.

3. People just don't want to change their accountant

Well we all know that's not really true don't we?

If we think it through, it would indicate the almost no firm would ever grow because people never change.

People change all the time though don't they?

Perhaps a truer revision of that statement would be 'People have not seen enough value or reason to change from their accountant to our practice to cancel out the hassle and guilt they feel about changing from a firm they have been with for years, regardless of the quality of service they receive.'

It's human nature for us to blame other factors or people for things not happening the way we want to. Rarely do we point the finger at ourselves and resolve to do something about it.

The reality is, it's in our hands and if reason number 2 ('we don't know how to') is being addressed, this reason number three vanishes from our vocabulary.

The reality is, it's in our hands and if reason number 2 ('we don't know how to') is being addressed, this reason number 3 vanishes from our vocabulary.

Investing in understanding what and why people buy is something that most firms do at some point. Implementing what they learn, reviewing and improving their knowledge and ability on a regular basis is what puts them ahead of 95% of every firm they will ever come up against to win new work because that failure to implement and improve is where 95% of accounting firms fail in their business development efforts.

There are specific, non-threatening ways of increasing a client's understanding of the value we offer to them and non-pressurised ways of giving them the opportunity to take advantage of this value without them feeling cajoled to buy.

The summary steps then to ensure businesses change to your firm when they are not referred to you.

1. Understand your prospect and their business.
2. Understand your own value as it relates to them and their business.
3. Link the two according to the prospective client's goals for being in business.
4. Take objections as encouragement that they care and are considering using your firm.
5. Earn the right to ask for their business by handling each objection patiently. If all objections have been resolved to the client's satisfaction, there is only one answer they can give.

Where are we taking our firms this year, down the 5% road of learning and implementing or the 95% road of learning or less?

4. We don't want to upset the client's relationship with us

This reason seems to be trotted out whenever a firm contemplates increasing the level of service to an existing client and getting paid for it. According to the number three reason however, people don't change their accountants so there's nothing to lose by approaching them on additional services right?

Because existing client revenue is the bedrock of every firm's ability to meet their mortgages, overhead, payroll etc. the reticence here is easy to understand.

There are specific, non-threatening ways though, of increasing a client's understanding of the value we offer to them and non-pressurised ways of giving them the opportunity to take advantage of this value without them feeling cajoled to buy.

It is that commitment to learning the skill set required to do this which will set our practices on our way to increasing existing client revenues, sometimes quite dramatically.

The more we delve into common reasons for things not getting done, the more we understand that the heart of these matters is the central belief system and skill set that the practice/individual subscribes to. Often they are 'self-limiting' beliefs and can only be changed by being challenged.

Who in the firm can perform that exercise?

5. We're unsure and don't know where or how to begin

Bingo.

There's every reason to be cautious about trying to develop something that requires us to become accomplished in areas that are currently unfamiliar to us, especially with the time investment required.

There's every reason to be cautious about trying to develop something that requires us to become accomplished in areas that are currently unfamiliar to us, especially with the time investment required.

If this is the case with you and your firm, you're one of the few who are being true to yourselves and facing reality. If you'd like to remove the fear of the unknown by doing something other than ignoring what needs to be done, it really is just a case of taking steps 'little and often' to learn the skill set possessed by an accomplished business developer and try to implement that stage by stage until you feel comfortable; before moving onto the next level of development.

That means that when your website offers services that you can't/have never provided, they don't really differentiate you. The combination of your emotional investment and the true extent of the support and assistance that you can provide is your actual differentiator.

This need to be 'all things to all businesses' often focuses us on telling our potential client everything that we can do and distracts us from building enough rapport and trust to have them feel comfortable in admitting what they actually want us to do.

So in order to become a commercially aware practice leader, we need to understand the DNA of leadership.

—

If you'd like to remove the fear of the unknown by doing something other than ignoring what needs to be done, it really is just a case of taking steps 'little and often' to learn the skill set...

The DNA of a practice leader

"Any woman or man leading an accounting firm, who chooses to overcome each operational or client challenge as it if their future depended on it, will not only succeed in practice but will become capable of delivering advisory value to their clients unmatched by their competitors; thus achieving true differentiation."

There has been enough behavioural evidence in practice management now observed, collated and reported upon, to be able to draw a conclusion that a great leader needs to be at peace internally in order to become a great leader externally. Her or his personnel/staff need to see a consistency between that leader's values and their most commonly perceived behaviours.

There has been enough behavioural evidence in practice management now observed, collated and reported upon, to be able to draw a conclusion that a great leader needs to be at peace internally in order to become a great leader externally

I recall a tremendous example seen on the Tottenham Court Road in London back in the early nineties. The scene is an electronic goods store where the owner had idol-esque status from employees and customers alike. He achieved that by building an empire from the ground up (the archetypal entrepreneur who started with nothing) whilst treating employees like partners in the business in terms of responsibility and reward, from the very beginning.

The myth and legend surrounding that owner had grown out of proportion and yet whenever I sat with him as a supplier to his business; he was humble, enthusiastic but devoid of any apparent ego.

I happened to be in store during the rise of a major dispute between an obnoxious sounding customer making a fairly insignificant purchase; and a store employee who was unquestionably 'in the right'.

As the argument escalated, the store owner quickly saw a number of threats to his business including the potential knock-on repercussions, depending how this situation was resolved, with potential lost income from other customers currently in store.

His act was swift and simple. He approached the store employee, thanked him by handshake for dealing with the situation to this point, before introducing himself to the irate customer and in gentle tones, taking the sting out of the complainant whilst walking him out of the store with arm placed non-threateningly over his shoulder.

Simple enough, had it ended there. However, once the patron was out of the store, the owner then returned, apologised to all other customers in store and with a cheeky grin added 'Our customers are always right….except that one'.

This got a laugh all around which removed any lingering awkwardness, but then with the crowd still watching, he approached the store employee involved in the original dispute; told him how well he felt he'd handled the customer and immediately made him employee of the month (where such a program carried considerable gravitas in terms of its rewards and chances for promotion)

Who in that high end central London shop is now left anything other than impressed with a millionaire store owner, whom in 5 minutes has demonstrated a willingness to work at the front end, diffuse a potentially damaging situation and congratulate/motivate an employee without giving anything away commercially in order to achieve it?

Who in that high end central London shop is now left anything other than impressed with a millionaire store owner, whom in 5 minutes has demonstrated a willingness to work at the front end...

I asked the owner how he continually demonstrates such a cheery disposition in these circumstances and almost flippantly he looked me in the eye and replied 'What's the alternative?'

Observations on creating an 'Upward Spiral'

Unhappy and difficult clients help our firms to improve our client management skills and present opportunities to refine our leadership skills.

It is tough for us to build a successful firm without difficult clients or internal personnel issues in order to provide learning experiences for us to build a robust and commercially successful infrastructure.

> It is tough for us to build a successful firm without difficult clients or internal personnel issues in order to provide learning experiences for us to build a robust and commercially successful infrastructure.

If we succeed in passing through the complaints, the breakaway group of professionals who set up in competition, the systems failures, the increasing legislation and regulation, the talented but naive employee who wants everything now, the untalented manager who sees the weakness in everyone but themselves, the major client leaving due to a lack of 'great service' and do it all with our integrity undiminished; we may expect at the close of each of these issues, to feel a measure of increased confidence, competence and enthusiasm about our eventual successful exit from the practice according to our aspirations.

How else, would we earn the right to successfully exit the firm as others before us had we not innovated and improved on what was an already firm foundation of processes and values in the organisation?

There is no other way in which the Managing and Senior Partners can make professional improvement and be prepared to pass the firm onto the next generation; than through the successful handling of these daily challenges.

Those daily challenges provide the increase in skill, knowledge and assuredness that allows us to develop new skill sets and new value to benefit ourselves, our senior managers and our clients with.

It could be demonstrated that when all is peaceful and prosperous with strong cash balances and no desire to grow the firm, leaders become indifferent and apathetic. Indeed we see that attitudes towards the urgency of developing 21st century sales and marketing disciplines in-house is hamstrung by the comfort blanket of recurring fees which remove the need to 'hunt and kill' each month in order to make rent and payroll, like the clients we profess to advise.

A few of our clients benefit from solid forecast-able repeat sales in the way we do, yet we are supposed to be able to advise them on the growth of their business and empathise with their situation in order to build relationships with them and potential other clients.

As we remain committed, problems, issues and challenges ultimately have a way of identifying their own solutions due to the openness and spirit of those tasked with solving them.

Our need, as counter intuitive as it might appear on the first read-through, is to constantly be challenging ourselves and evaluating our attitudes towards the issues that might bore us senseless in our practice this morning. What do we believe about ourselves and our abilities in terms of solving problems and progressing the practice? Our beliefs govern our behaviours.

When we develop a resolve to continually overcome practice challenges, we demonstrate to our people that we are interested in the success of the organisation more than we are interested in self-preservation. This increases loyalty, emotional buy-in and the steadfastness of those who might be funding our retirement in years to come.

As we remain committed, problems, issues and challenges ultimately have a way of identifying their own solutions due to the openness and spirit of those tasked with solving them.

As twee as it sounds, Chin-up! Don't allow disheartenment to defeat you because your choice to not be defeated, guarantees your eventual victory over the issues you face in the first place.

Who is the sort of leader that you, yourself would want to be? Who is the sort of leader that those whom you lead would be inspired by? What are the beliefs, attitudes and behaviours required to become that leader? Do you have the desire to go through all that to become that person consistently?

If we can forecast anything in our businesses, we can forecast challenges and the choice of how to react to them. Victory over the systems, client issues and internal people issues we face earns us the right to look back on those difficult times and acknowledge that this is when we developed ourselves as leaders the most.

If we can forecast anything in our businesses, we can forecast challenges and the choice of how to react to them.

When we contemplate how fortunate we are to have been elevated or to have built ourselves and our firm to the level that we now enjoy, it may be that the journey we've been on has not always been the most pleasant with blood pressure heightened, sleep lost and appetite diminished.

How many of us though, have realised afterwards that those circumstances which have been so very unpleasant, have often proved of the highest advantage to us and our firm's improvement?

How far have we advanced, how much knowledge have we obtained and how much more are we able to deal with now both internally and on behalf of our clients now than we were one, two or five years ago?

When we were children, we grew up and got stronger without knowing how it was happening. When we build muscle, we have to expand it and increase the blood flow that we can get through it.

So it is with the developing leader. The sacrifices and difficulties faced with the range of very real and seemingly insurmountable emotions that they present are actually our opportunity to grow and develop.

If the appetite is not there, even grudgingly, to face those challenges head on with the hope of victory beyond the immediate horizon, will the firm grow and bluntly, should you placed be in charge of it?

Partnership pointers

1. Take time to identify a leader you admire from any walk of life. Jot down a criterion for emulating their success behaviours. How many of these criteria do you fulfil yourself already and what do you yet lack but can work on right away?
2. Why do so many of us have negative, fearful or defeatist outlooks? How many of those types of people have become great leaders inside or outside of the accounting profession? How do you avoid succumbing to that same mind-set? You now know what you bring to your client relationships.
3. Pick two people you trust and admire; one from within the firm and one from outside. Ask them to describe the attributes or anatomy of a leader that impresses them. Then go about deciding how you will develop any of the traits and behaviours they've identified that you don't yet demonstrate on a perpetual basis.

The expert council

If you could give only one piece of advice to senior/managing partners right now, what would it be?

Become timeless. And I mean that in two ways. Just bite the bullet and ditch that damn weight around your neck that's drowning you and you think it's a life raft — the timesheet. Burn them, bury them.

And I mean timeless in the other way too — make what you do timeless inasmuch as you're focussed on leaving a legacy not of consumption but one of contribution.

Paul Dunn
Chairman B1G1

Get these bits right:

- *Understand the strategic issues affecting the profession*
- *Keep your clients*
- *Develop your personal selling skills*
- *Know the importance of practice management with regard to chargeable time, Lock up and invoicing*
- *Cultivate leadership and working with the team*
- *Get cross selling and value pricing right*
- *Remember: action speaks louder than words*

Gordon Gilchrist
2020 Innovations

Whilst there is still a feeling of "I had to make my own way, so they can too" in some firms; there are also many partnerships now who are becoming very transparent in their expectations of new partners and crucially their admission processes. So people can figure out what they need to do.

At a personal level, the problem with many professionals is that they don't migrate and change their skill set fast enough as they grow in their careers – if the only thing you can do, or be, in your early or mid-30s is be a great accountant, then you must remember there are people who are just as good as you but 5 or 10 years younger and cheaper. If you don't change, you are left behind.

My advice is in three pieces – firstly go get a mentor – find someone you respect and ask if they will do the role for you. Secondly take your development seriously and manage it like the project it is. That project is called "My Career". Thirdly keep growing and reinventing yourself as a better and better advisor.

Mike Mister
Global Director of Executive Development
Ernst & Young Global

CONCLUSION ON
COMMERCIAL AWARENESS

The thing about Accountants is that they occupy, should they wish to, a unique position in the minds of their clients. We know it as most trusted advisor. Simply put, if you are a trusted advisor, you're supposed to be good at what you do, run your own business successfully and be well worth your fee.

Employee versus ownership

What makes you think you want to be a Partner?

What makes you think you're good enough to be considered for Partnership in your firm?

What was the average age that the current Partners reached their positions?

What types of challenges do they go through each day as a Partner?

What are the biggest lessons they've learned in their time as a Partner of the firm?
(Hint: invite them out to lunch to ask for their advice, counsel, direction and opinion)

What does the Partner you speak to the most think you lack before becoming Partner 'material'?

How long are you prepared to wait to be considered for Partnership before evaluating your options?

How did the Partner you speak to the most get their chance to move up in the firm?

Conclusion

The thing about Accountants is that they occupy, should they wish to, a unique position in the minds of their clients. We know it as most trusted advisor. Simply put, if you are a trusted advisor, you're supposed to be good at what you do, run your own business successfully and be well worth your fee. On the presumption that all of the above are true, please, for me, can we please stop?

- The needless discounting and low balling of quotes as if you wouldn't get the engagement if it were priced correctly and so prefer to create a false and detrimental impression of your worth right from the outset.
- Discounting when a new piece of work is required by a client. If we're asked to do extra work, the client presumably rates us for the work already done. Reflect that value in the fee.
- Discounting when a client disputes the bill. Did you set realistic expectations at the start? Good, charge full value. What are they going to do, leave? If we've you sprung the bill on them, no wonder they're annoyed, in which case discount and feel lucky to have kept them. Don't make that mistake again.
- Saying accountants are boring in an ironic self-acknowledgement of the commonly held myth surrounding the profession. You're not boring and by trying to curry favour by employing self-deprecating humour we're just perpetuating the myth. Don't perpetuate it, disprove it.
- Hiring marketing support staff that know nothing about professional services and have no track record. It's unlikely that what worked in their last role in wine retail will work for 'trusted advisors'. The appointment will cost money, not create it.

- Taking six weeks to get back to a potential new client after the initial meeting. The excuse 'we're so busy', doesn't tell the client that our firm is in demand; it tells them that they are likely to receive a service as crappy as the one they are getting when they are supposed to be in this 'courting' phase with us.
- Saying you convert 95% of opportunities once your foot is in the door. You're talking about referrals and we all convert 95% of those. Marketing brings about non-referred opportunities, ones that we have to sweat to get but would've been unlikely to have gotten any other way. 25% of those converted is good going initially.
- Claiming low client attrition rates as a barometer of great service. No-one moves accountants unless they need to and very few know why they need to because they are not educated very well by competing firms. Our clients are perpetually at risk, minimise the liability with actual good service as in, what the clients values about us rather than what we think is good about us.
- The political in-fighting with your peer level colleagues. This is a team game.

And now that I've got that off my chest...

Please start understanding, valuing and respecting your own value in the marketplace with clients who could not reach their goals without you. Businesses are in need, sometimes desperate need of your technical expertise and caring approach. Take that to them instead because, speaking as one who is looked after well myself, we love it and we are prepared to pay a premium without ever asking for discounts.

In closing...

Passport to Partnership started as an idea several years ago and has turned into a curriculum, a standard, several guidebooks, DVDs, online and audio programs.

I didn't envisage such a grand destiny for the concept so there is proof, if any were required, that ambitious career goals are always within reach.

However, I've received even more fulfillment from meeting each of you. I've been able to learn about your careers, your ambitions and your altruistic desire to do what is best and what is right for your firm and your clients.

That altruistic spirit is largely missing from accounting, which was once termed a 'noble profession' and has now been relegated to a mere 'industry'. I challenge you to bring that altruistic spirit back as you rise to the leadership positions that you're no doubt destined for.

The very best of luck to you in your careers, although if you can mark each of the application form questions in this book with the answer "Clear strength", I don't think you're going to need it!

PASSPORT TO PARTNERSHIP

PERSONAL PROGRESS PLAN & WORKBOOK

APPENDIX

BONUS DOWNLOAD INSTRUCTIONS

To download the materials in this Appendix, go to:

https://store.cpatrendlines.com/?p=368

Your password is:

passport

PERSONAL PURPOSE CHECKLIST

Which of these factors below on a scale of 1-10 (1 = not important at all, 10 = vital) truly gets you out of bed each morning on a consistent basis?

FACTOR	RATING									
Being a part of the firm	1	2	3	4	5	6	7	8	9	10
Professional ambition	1	2	3	4	5	6	7	8	9	10
Taking on challenges	1	2	3	4	5	6	7	8	9	10
Having control over your future	1	2	3	4	5	6	7	8	9	10
Autonomy	1	2	3	4	5	6	7	8	9	10
Family needs	1	2	3	4	5	6	7	8	9	10
Recognition	1	2	3	4	5	6	7	8	9	10
Sense of unity	1	2	3	4	5	6	7	8	9	10
Creating a legacy	1	2	3	4	5	6	7	8	9	10
Parental acknowledgment	1	2	3	4	5	6	7	8	9	10
Acquisition of knowledge	1	2	3	4	5	6	7	8	9	10
Being an example	1	2	3	4	5	6	7	8	9	10
Making a difference	1	2	3	4	5	6	7	8	9	10
Responsibility	1	2	3	4	5	6	7	8	9	10
Power	1	2	3	4	5	6	7	8	9	10
Serving the clients	1	2	3	4	5	6	7	8	9	10
Advancement	1	2	3	4	5	6	7	8	9	10
Feeling needed	1	2	3	4	5	6	7	8	9	10
Ethical responsibility	1	2	3	4	5	6	7	8	9	10

THE SEVEN Cs OF PARTNERSHIP

Name all seven of the seven Cs

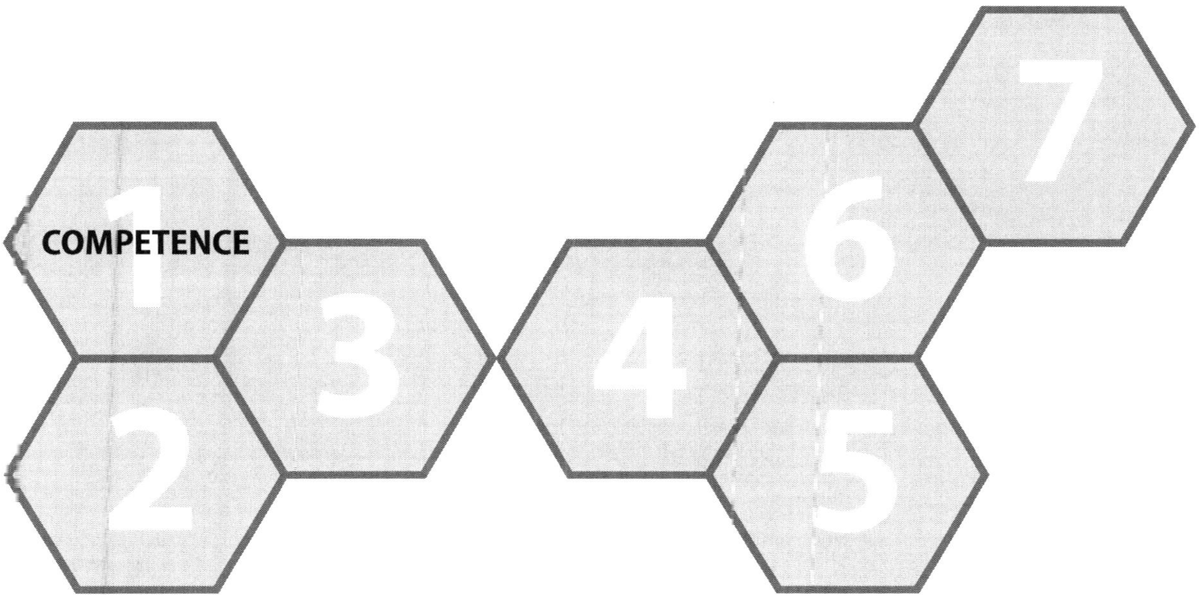

1. COMPETENCE
2.
3.
4.
5.
6.
7.

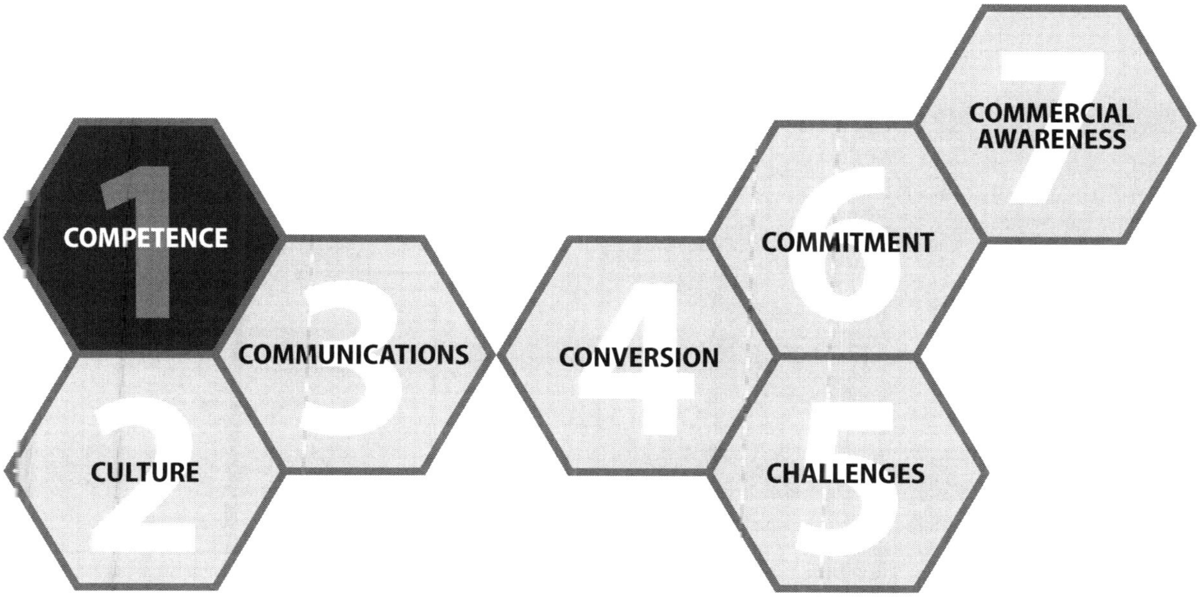
1 COMPETENCE
2 CULTURE
3 COMMUNICATIONS
4 CONVERSION
5 CHALLENGES
6 COMMITMENT
7 COMMERCIAL AWARENESS

THE FIRST 'C' — COMPETENCE

STARTING POINT

Fill in the sections below to establish your starting point for career growth.

MY AMBITIONS

What are your career ambitions for the next one to five years?

Earnings ambitions

Life balance ambitions

Type of projects worked on, niche specialisms developed, free time available etc.

Achievements to obtain

Make Partner, start own firm, be recognized for my work, get involved with Charity work etc.

Why do you want to achieve these things specifically?

The most motivational reason is…

The impact of not achieving these things is…

What will you and those closest to you feel like when you've achieved them? How will that day play out?

THE FIRST 'C' — COMPETENCE

STARTING POINT

Fill in the sections below to establish your starting point for career growth.

FINANCIAL OUTLINE

One year from today, what figure would you like your annual salary to have reached?

What is your current salary and how long have you been at that level?

What justification could you give to your firm to support the required increase?

Currently underpaid compared to peer-level elsewhere, in line with rate of inflation, advance against future business brought in etc.

What additional return on investment could you demonstrate to justify the increase?

Extra responsibility, removal of headaches from Partner's workload, self-investment in rainmaking training etc.

Based on these parameters, what do you need to do before you can be successful in achieving this raise?

What areas of weakness have you identified that you need to put right before justifying this raise and what is your plan for doing so and by when?

THE FIRST 'C' — COMPETENCE

PARTNERSHIP POINTERS

Ask yourself and answer these questions when considering your 'competence' as a leader.

1. What were the greatest challenges that the partners of my firm faced in their careers and how did they handle it?

2. What are the three main traits that my partners are looking for in a leader of our firm?

3. If a Partner saw all my online activity, would their opinion of my suitability for leadership be altered, either way?

THE FIRST 'C' CHECKLIST

COMPETENCE

Does my work demonstrate a high level of technical ability?

- ☐ 1 Clear strength: "One of the things I do best"
- ☐ 2 Hidden strength: "Others rate me higher than I do"
- ☐ 3 Blind spot: "I rate myself higher than others do"
- ☐ 4 Weakness: "I don't do this well"
- ☐ 5 Untested area: "I don't know enough to answer this question"
- ☐ 6 Don't know: "I need more feedback"

Do I share my knowledge and experience with other members of my team?

- ☐ 1 Clear strength: "One of the things I do best"
- ☐ 2 Hidden strength: "Others rate me higher than I do"
- ☐ 3 Blind spot: "I rate myself higher than others do"
- ☐ 4 Weakness: "I don't do this well"
- ☐ 5 Untested area: "I don't know enough to answer this question"
- ☐ 6 Don't know: "I need more feedback"

Does my competence stretch to managing people?

- ☐ 1 Clear strength: "One of the things I do best"
- ☐ 2 Hidden strength: "Others rate me higher than I do"
- ☐ 3 Blind spot: "I rate myself higher than others do"
- ☐ 4 Weakness: "I don't do this well"
- ☐ 5 Untested area: "I don't know enough to answer this question"
- ☐ 6 Don't know: "I need more feedback"

Do I understand all the ares that the Partners want me to demonstrate my competence in?

- ☐ 1 Clear strength: "One of the things I do best"
- ☐ 2 Hidden strength: "Others rate me higher than I do"
- ☐ 3 Blind spot: "I rate myself higher than others do"
- ☐ 4 Weakness: "I don't do this well"
- ☐ 5 Untested area: "I don't know enough to answer this question"
- ☐ 6 Don't know: "I need more feedback"

Have I got a wide breadth of competence in a range of disciplines performed by my firm?

- ☐ 1 Clear strength: "One of the things I do best"
- ☐ 2 Hidden strength: "Others rate me higher than I do"
- ☐ 3 Blind spot: "I rate myself higher than others do"
- ☐ 4 Weakness: "I don't do this well"
- ☐ 5 Untested area: "I don't know enough to answer this question"
- ☐ 6 Don't know: "I need more feedback"

THE FIRST 'C' — COMPETENCE

PERFECTING THE PERSONAL BRAND

What are the major characteristics that your colleagues would use to describe you if put on the spot?

What are the major characteristics that your Partners would use to describe you if put on the spot?

Is there any discrepancy between the two? What do you need to correct, if anything?

What are the main examples of your command of the 1st C (Competence) that your Partners have seen you demonstrate in your roles in the firm?

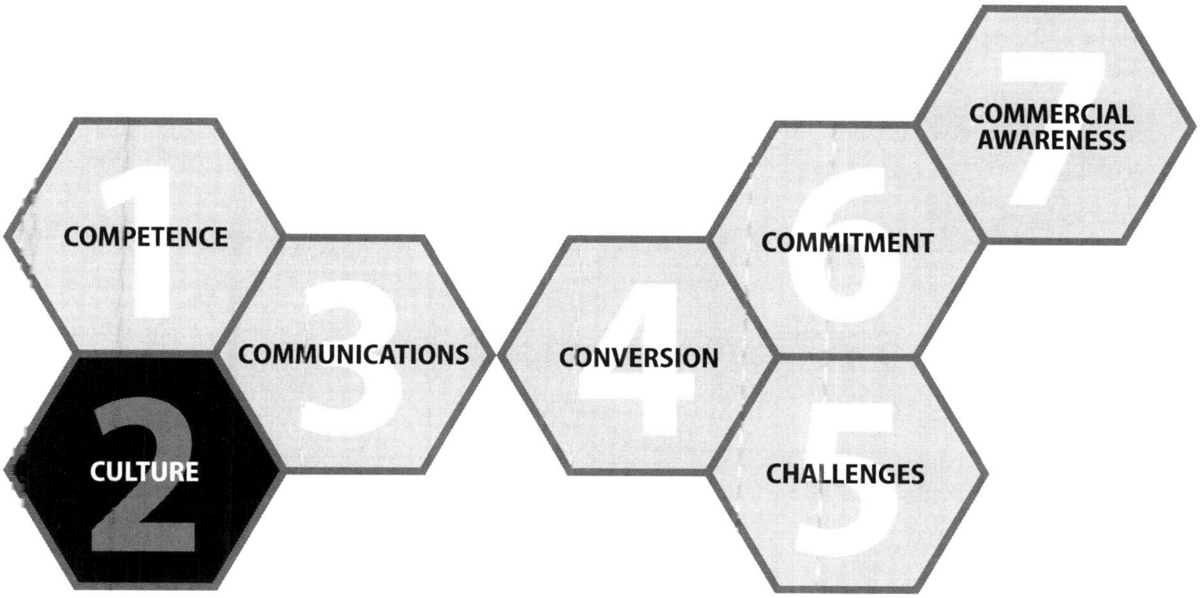
COMPETENCE
1
CULTURE
2
COMMUNICATIONS
3
CONVERSION
4
CHALLENGES
5
COMMITMENT
6
COMMERCIAL AWARENESS
7

THE SECOND 'C' — CULTURE

PARTNERSHIP POINTERS

Ask yourself and answer these questions when considering the current and future 'Culture' of your firm.

1. Partner disagreements must have happened in the past at my firm. Without naming names, what did the Managing Partner do about it? Could I handle things that way myself?

2. What do the partners see as culturally critical to the identity of the firm?

3. If I spend all my time rallying against perceived injustices in the way my firm is run, I'm going to be viewed as small fry forever. One way in which I can overcome that sense of injustice is.....

THE SECOND 'C' CHECKLIST

CULTURE

Do I earn the respect of the partners in my firm?

- ☐ 1 Clear strength: "One of the things I do best"
- ☐ 2 Hidden strength: "Others rate me higher than I do"
- ☐ 3 Blind spot: "I rate myself higher than others do"
- ☐ 4 Weakness: "I don't do this well"
- ☐ 5 Untested area: "I don't know enough to answer this question"
- ☐ 6 Don't know: "I need more feedback"

Do I earn the respect of my colleagues in the firm?

- ☐ 1 Clear strength: "One of the things I do best"
- ☐ 2 Hidden strength: "Others rate me higher than I do"
- ☐ 3 Blind spot: "I rate myself higher than others do"
- ☐ 4 Weakness: "I don't do this well"
- ☐ 5 Untested area: "I don't know enough to answer this question"
- ☐ 6 Don't know: "I need more feedback"

Can I identify who to ask to obtain ongoing confidential feedback on the above?

- ☐ 1 Clear strength: "One of the things I do best"
- ☐ 2 Hidden strength: "Others rate me higher than I do"
- ☐ 3 Blind spot: "I rate myself higher than others do"
- ☐ 4 Weakness: "I don't do this well"
- ☐ 5 Untested area: "I don't know enough to answer this question"
- ☐ 6 Don't know: "I need more feedback"

How well do I observe the unwritten rules of this firm?

- ☐ 1 Clear strength: "One of the things I do best"
- ☐ 2 Hidden strength: "Others rate me higher than I do"
- ☐ 3 Blind spot: "I rate myself higher than others do"
- ☐ 4 Weakness: "I don't do this well"
- ☐ 5 Untested area: "I don't know enough to answer this question"
- ☐ 6 Don't know: "I need more feedback"

How accomplished am I at not taking sides in matters of office politics?

- ☐ 1 Clear strength: "One of the things I do best"
- ☐ 2 Hidden strength: "Others rate me higher than I do"
- ☐ 3 Blind spot: "I rate myself higher than others do"
- ☐ 4 Weakness: "I don't do this well"
- ☐ 5 Untested area: "I don't know enough to answer this question"
- ☐ 6 Don't know: "I need more feedback"

THE SECOND 'C' — CULTURE

SEVEN LEVELS OF COMMUNICATION MANAGEMENT

Name the seven levels of communication management

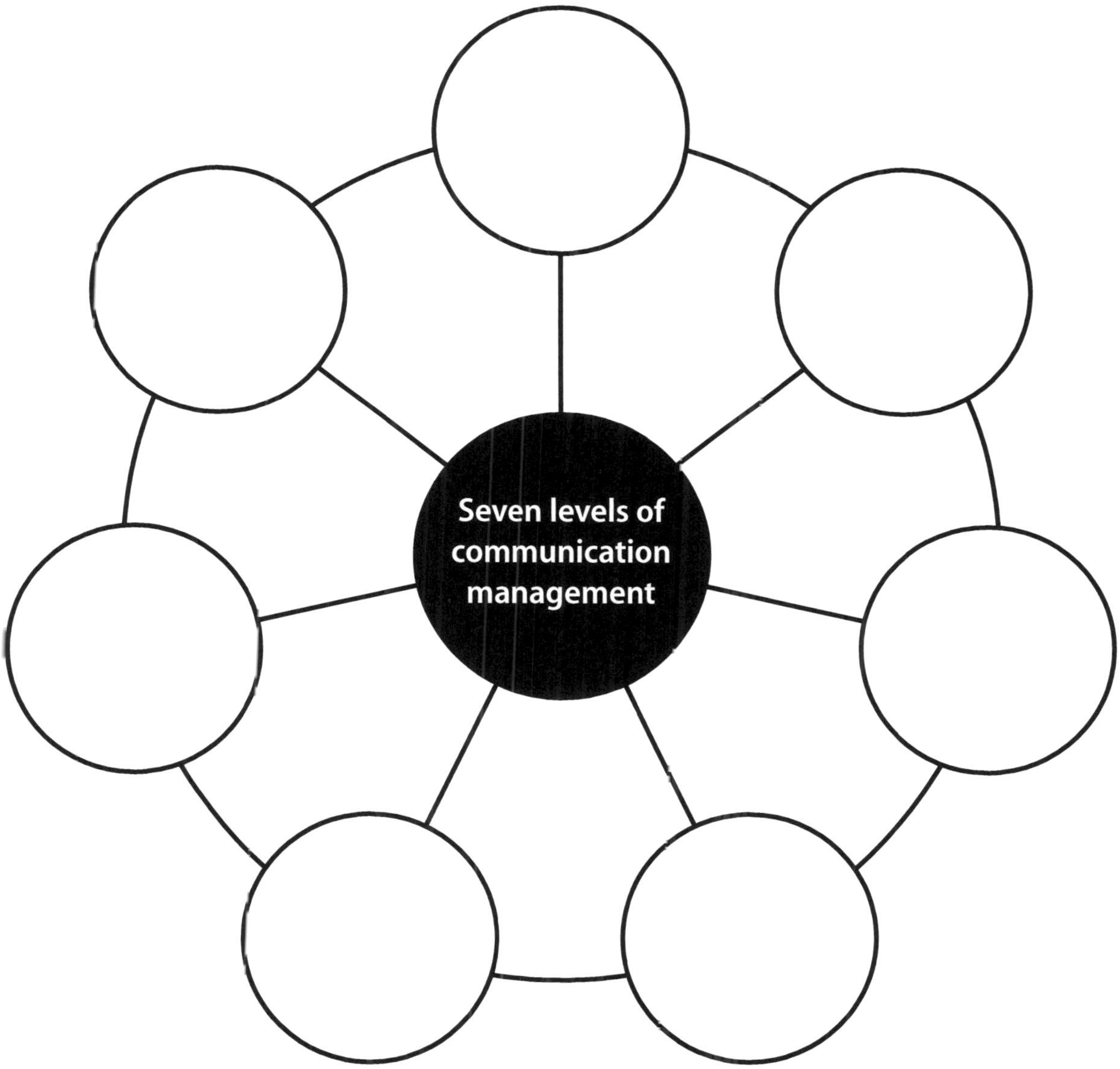

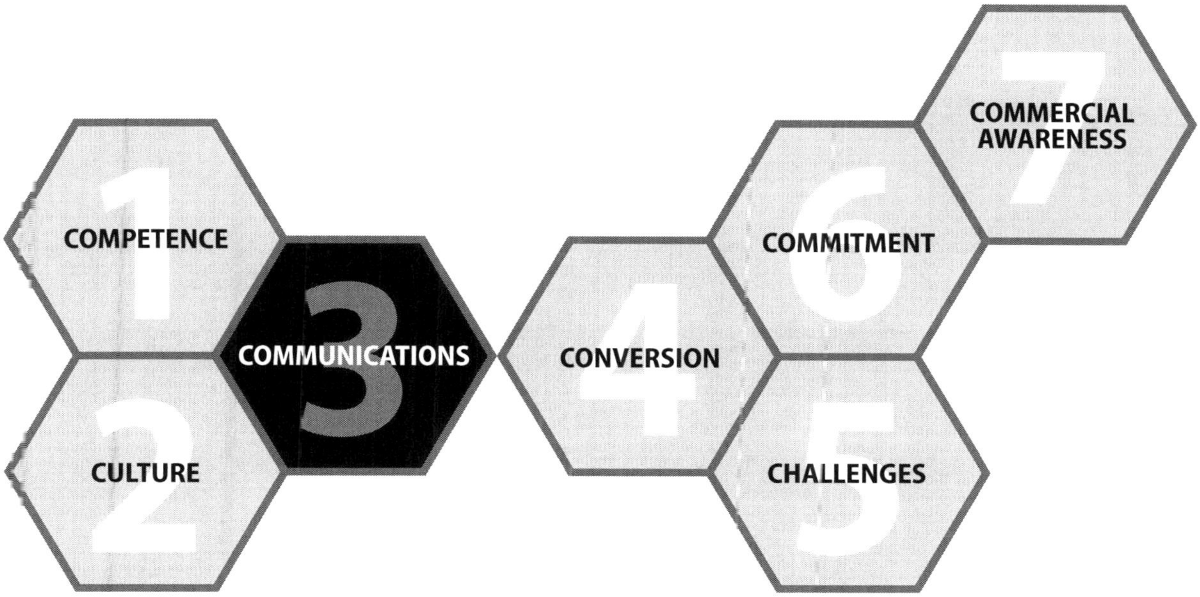
1
COMPETENCE
2
CULTURE
3
COMMUNICATIONS
4
CONVERSION
5
CHALLENGES
6
COMMITMENT
7
COMMERCIAL AWARENESS

THE THIRD 'C' — COMMUNICATION

PARTNERSHIP POINTERS

Ask yourself and answer these questions when considering the current and future 'Communication' tactics that you'll employ.

1. If I was my client, boss, peer or subordinate, how would I want to be communicated with by me?

2. What areas of my firm's communication can I improve quickly?

3. I need to understand that it does not matter how I think I'm coming across. I need to understand how the person I'm communicating with thinks I'm coming across.

THE THIRD 'C' — COMMUNICATION

MY WORTH

Directions for defining your worth

1. Review your firm's ambitions, ethos, challenges and service line gaps.
2. Based on these, identify the value you bring to your firm and its clients.
3. Rate each area of value from 1(low) to 5 (high) for the outcomes delivered to the client/your firm, how exclusive this area is to you, and the strength of the proof you have for it.

COMPONENTS OF MY WORTH TO THE FIRM

COMPONENTS	OUTCOMES	UNIQUENESS	EVIDENCE
e.g. tax expertise	*Savings*	*4*	*Case Studies*

THE THIRD 'C' — COMMUNICATION

WHY AM I VALUABLE?

Directions

1. Based on your selected components, prove your value in a sentence.
2. Create a 1-3 sentence summary.
3. Create 3-5 bullet points to expand and add evidence to the summary.
4. Run them by a trusted colleague until the consensus is that they are well honed.

My value in a sentence:

My value in overview format:

My evidence:

THE THIRD 'C' — COMMUNICATION

EXTERNAL COMMUNICATION SOCIAL MEDIA PROFILES

Professional headline

Based on the My Value section

What type of clients do you work with?

What outcomes do they get from working with you?

What's a simple statement of why they choose you over the competition?

THE THIRD 'C' — COMMUNICATION

SUMMARY

Reiterate who you work with and how you help them.

Expand on the outcomes they see in working with you – provide evidence.

Provide evidence that you can do what you say you can.
(Examples of client results, testimonials, case studies, awards, etc.)

Give them a reason to get in touch with you.
(Examples of free report, consultation, seminar invite etc)

THE THIRD 'C' CHECKLIST

COMMUNICATION

How well do I communicate vital information on time to the Partners?

- ☐ 1 Clear strength: "One of the things I do best"
- ☐ 2 Hidden strength: "Others rate me higher than I do"
- ☐ 3 Blind spot: "I rate myself higher than others do"
- ☐ 4 Weakness: "I don't do this well"
- ☐ 5 Untested area: "I don't know enough to answer this question"
- ☐ 6 Don't know: "I need more feedback"

How well do I communicate to clients the work I'm doing for them and its impact?

- ☐ 1 Clear strength: "One of the things I do best"
- ☐ 2 Hidden strength: "Others rate me higher than I do"
- ☐ 3 Blind spot: "I rate myself higher than others do"
- ☐ 4 Weakness: "I don't do this well"
- ☐ 5 Untested area: "I don't know enough to answer this question"
- ☐ 6 Don't know: "I need more feedback"

How well do I communicate what I require and why to my team?

- ☐ 1 Clear strength: "One of the things I do best"
- ☐ 2 Hidden strength: "Others rate me higher than I do"
- ☐ 3 Blind spot: "I rate myself higher than others do"
- ☐ 4 Weakness: "I don't do this well"
- ☐ 5 Untested area: "I don't know enough to answer this question"
- ☐ 6 Don't know: "I need more feedback"

How well do I build relationships with external influencers?

- ☐ 1 Clear strength: "One of the things I do best"
- ☐ 2 Hidden strength: "Others rate me higher than I do"
- ☐ 3 Blind spot: "I rate myself higher than others do"
- ☐ 4 Weakness: "I don't do this well"
- ☐ 5 Untested area: "I don't know enough to answer this question"
- ☐ 6 Don't know: "I need more feedback"

If I was asked by a potential client today "Why should I join your firm?" how well can I communicate the value we can deliver for our clients at this practice?

- ☐ 1 Clear strength: "One of the things I do best"
- ☐ 2 Hidden strength: "Others rate me higher than I do"
- ☐ 3 Blind spot: "I rate myself higher than others do"
- ☐ 4 Weakness: "I don't do this well"
- ☐ 5 Untested area: "I don't know enough to answer this question"
- ☐ 6 Don't know: "I need more feedback"

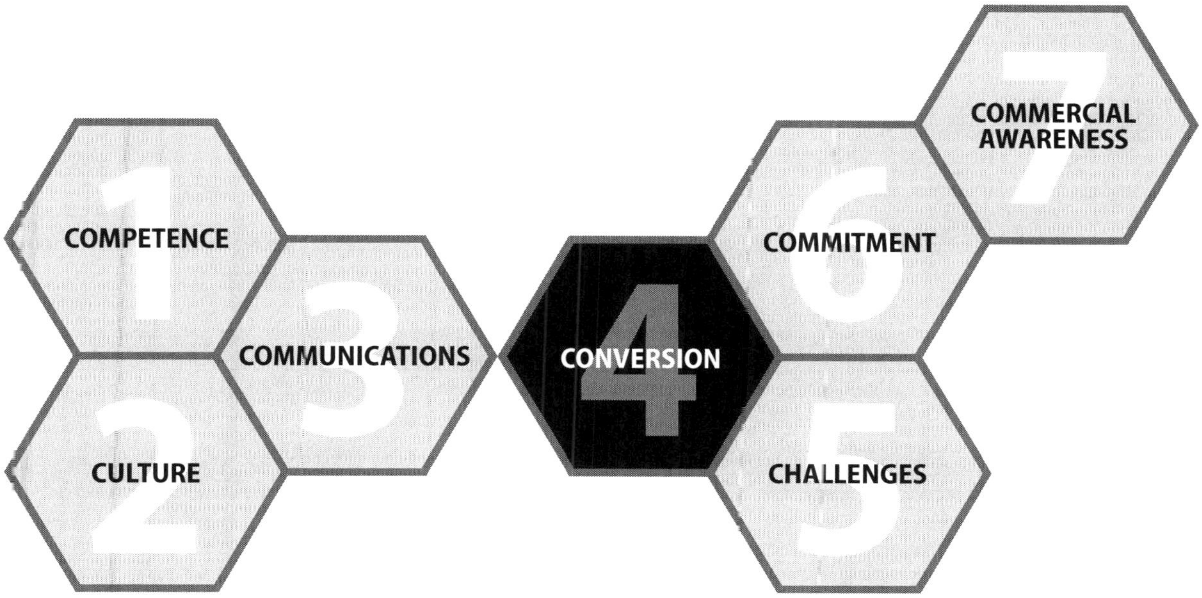
COMPETENCE
CULTURE
COMMUNICATIONS
CONVERSION
COMMITMENT
CHALLENGES
COMMERCIAL AWARENESS

THE FOURTH 'C' — CONVERSION

PARTNERSHIP POINTERS

Ask yourself and answer these questions when considering the current and future 'Conversion' tactics that you'll employ.

1. If I was to start today, could I name 4 businesses that I'd like to reach out to?

2. What is our firm's net fee growth goal this year and what can I do to contribute to it?

3. What do I need to do to be able to handle the tough stuff like negotiation, pricing and handling objections? What start to learning these skills can I make today?

THE FOURTH 'C' CHECKLIST

CONVERSION

Do I have my own pipeline of potential clients?

- ☐ 1 Clear strength: "One of the things I do best"
- ☐ 2 Hidden strength: "Others rate me higher than I do"
- ☐ 3 Blind spot: "I rate myself higher than others do"
- ☐ 4 Weakness: "I don't do this well"
- ☐ 5 Untested area: "I don't know enough to answer this question"
- ☐ 6 Don't know: "I need more feedback"

Do I have my own LinkedIn profile?

- ☐ 1 Clear strength: "One of the things I do best"
- ☐ 2 Hidden strength: "Others rate me higher than I do"
- ☐ 3 Blind spot: "I rate myself higher than others do"
- ☐ 4 Weakness: "I don't do this well"
- ☐ 5 Untested area: "I don't know enough to answer this question"
- ☐ 6 Don't know: "I need more feedback"

Am I connected to introducers of new work?

- ☐ 1 Clear strength: "One of the things I do best"
- ☐ 2 Hidden strength: "Others rate me higher than I do"
- ☐ 3 Blind spot: "I rate myself higher than others do"
- ☐ 4 Weakness: "I don't do this well"
- ☐ 5 Untested area: "I don't know enough to answer this question"
- ☐ 6 Don't know: "I need more feedback"

How good do I think I am in converting non-referred opportunities into fee paying clients?

- ☐ 1 Clear strength: "One of the things I do best"
- ☐ 2 Hidden strength: "Others rate me higher than I do"
- ☐ 3 Blind spot: "I rate myself higher than others do"
- ☐ 4 Weakness: "I don't do this well"
- ☐ 5 Untested area: "I don't know enough to answer this question"
- ☐ 6 Don't know: "I need more feedback"

How good am I at handling objections such as when a client questions our fees?

- ☐ 1 Clear strength: "One of the things I do best"
- ☐ 2 Hidden strength: "Others rate me higher than I do"
- ☐ 3 Blind spot: "I rate myself higher than others do"
- ☐ 4 Weakness: "I don't do this well"
- ☐ 5 Untested area: "I don't know enough to answer this question"
- ☐ 6 Don't know: "I need more feedback"

THE FOURTH 'C' — CONVERSION

BUILDING YOUR PIPELINE

Record the businesses you'd ideally like to work with or believe you can add value to below, for future inclusion in your personal pipeline:

Next list any clients which the firm has lost that you feel you could realistically win back:

List any proposals that you were involved with that the firm didn't win. How many of those prospects found what they were looking for? Enter in your pipeline, any that you can't say for sure are happy with their current arrangements:

Detail any current clients that you believe your firm could add value to according to their needs and the services/outcomes that could be delivered:

THE FOURTH 'C' — CONVERSION

BUILDING YOUR PIPELINE

EVERYONE ELSE

List any other businesses that you know (friends, family etc) that you feel you could serve in a way that is superior to their current arrangements:

What 'Stories of Success' can you employ when reaching out to these businesses?

Allocate a conservative figure for the first year's fees that would be derived from winning the business that you've highlighted. What percentage of this figure would be required to justify the increase you desire in your compensation?

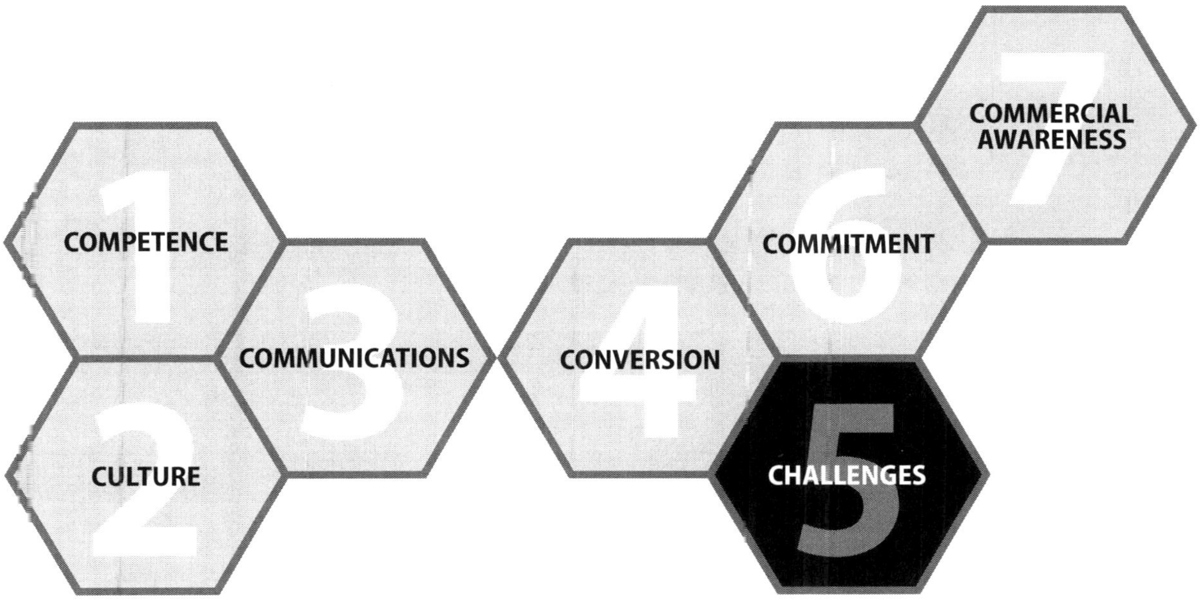
COMPETENCE
CULTURE
COMMUNICATIONS
CONVERSION
CHALLENGES
COMMITMENT
COMMERCIAL AWARENESS

THE FIFTH 'C' — COMMITMENT

PARTNERSHIP POINTERS

Ask yourself and answer these questions when considering the current and future 'Commitment' behaviours that you'll employ.

1. What is my first reaction to being asked to work outside of my normal hours?

2. How well do I understand the history and ethos of this firm and do I appreciate what the current partners have had to do to get this firm to where it can afford to pay me today?

3. Is my focus on my own progression at any cost or are my colleagues and their feelings and futures on my mind at the same time?

THE FIFTH 'C' CHECKLIST

COMMITMENT

Do I work extra hours without being asked?

- ☐ 1 Clear strength: "One of the things I do best"
- ☐ 2 Hidden strength: "Others rate me higher than I do"
- ☐ 3 Blind spot: "I rate myself higher than others do"
- ☐ 4 Weakness: "I don't do this well"
- ☐ 5 Untested area: "I don't know enough to answer this question"
- ☐ 6 Don't know: "I need more feedback"

Do I work extra hours without being paid?

- ☐ 1 Clear strength: "One of the things I do best"
- ☐ 2 Hidden strength: "Others rate me higher than I do"
- ☐ 3 Blind spot: "I rate myself higher than others do"
- ☐ 4 Weakness: "I don't do this well"
- ☐ 5 Untested area: "I don't know enough to answer this question"
- ☐ 6 Don't know: "I need more feedback"

Do I seem committed to the partners in my firm?

- ☐ 1 Clear strength: "One of the things I do best"
- ☐ 2 Hidden strength: "Others rate me higher than I do"
- ☐ 3 Blind spot: "I rate myself higher than others do"
- ☐ 4 Weakness: "I don't do this well"
- ☐ 5 Untested area: "I don't know enough to answer this question"
- ☐ 6 Don't know: "I need more feedback"

When work gets piled on me, do I act maturely in dealing with it?

- ☐ 1 Clear strength: "One of the things I do best"
- ☐ 2 Hidden strength: "Others rate me higher than I do"
- ☐ 3 Blind spot: "I rate myself higher than others do"
- ☐ 4 Weakness: "I don't do this well"
- ☐ 5 Untested area: "I don't know enough to answer this question"
- ☐ 6 Don't know: "I need more feedback"

Do I demonstrate that I'm working for the good of the firm ahead of the good of my career?

- ☐ 1 Clear strength: "One of the things I do best"
- ☐ 2 Hidden strength: "Others rate me higher than I do"
- ☐ 3 Blind spot: "I rate myself higher than others do"
- ☐ 4 Weakness: "I don't do this well"
- ☐ 5 Untested area: "I don't know enough to answer this question"
- ☐ 6 Don't know: "I need more feedback"

THE FOURTH 'C' — COMMITMENT

SHOWING YOUR TRUE COLORS

What kind of loyalty does the firm place a high value on?
For example working extra hours without being asked, informing them on competitor activity, making them aware of job offers you've received and rejected?

Based on what the Partners place a high value on, what commitment can you actively demonstrate to the firm on an ongoing basis?

Write down your shortlist of people in your team/department you feel that you can instill this same sense of commitment in and how you are going to go about it.

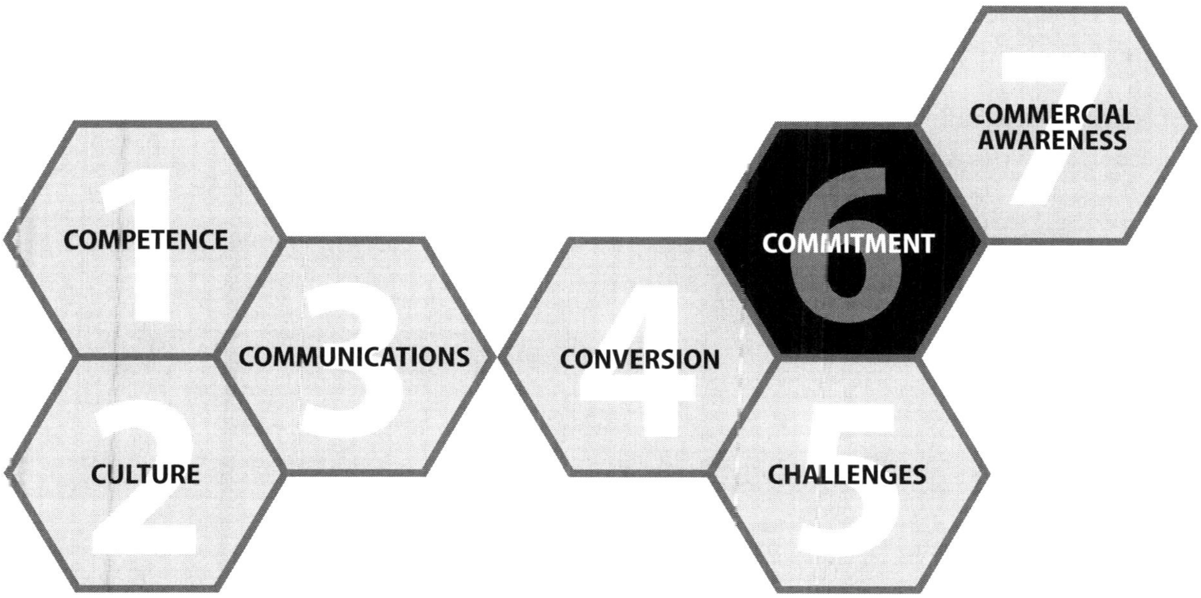
7
COMMERCIAL
AWARENESS
1
COMPETENCE
6
COMMITMENT
3
COMMUNICATIONS
4
CONVERSION
2
CULTURE
5
CHALLENGES

THE SIXTH 'C' — CHALLENGES

PARTNERSHIP POINTERS

Ask yourself and answer these questions when considering the current and future 'Challenges' behaviours that you'll employ.

1. What is my first reaction to being notified of a client complaint?

2. How well do I understand the role that everyone else plays in the firm, especially the challenges faced by its leadership?

3. Is my focus on making myself look good or solving issues for the firm and its clients as effectively and efficiently as I know how?

THE SIXTH 'C' CHECKLIST

CHALLENGES

How do I react to issues in my work day?

- ☐ 1 Clear strength: "One of the things I do best"
- ☐ 2 Hidden strength: "Others rate me higher than I do"
- ☐ 3 Blind spot: "I rate myself higher than others do"
- ☐ 4 Weakness: "I don't do this well"
- ☐ 5 Untested area: "I don't know enough to answer this question"
- ☐ 6 Don't know: "I need more feedback"

How fast do I weigh up the situation before speaking or taking action?

- ☐ 1 Clear strength: "One of the things I do best"
- ☐ 2 Hidden strength: "Others rate me higher than I do"
- ☐ 3 Blind spot: "I rate myself higher than others do"
- ☐ 4 Weakness: "I don't do this well"
- ☐ 5 Untested area: "I don't know enough to answer this question"
- ☐ 6 Don't know: "I need more feedback"

How well do I consider other people's opinions as well as my own?

- ☐ 1 Clear strength: "One of the things I do best"
- ☐ 2 Hidden strength: "Others rate me higher than I do"
- ☐ 3 Blind spot: "I rate myself higher than others do"
- ☐ 4 Weakness: "I don't do this well"
- ☐ 5 Untested area: "I don't know enough to answer this question"
- ☐ 6 Don't know: "I need more feedback"

How good is my track record of acting in the client's best interests?

- ☐ 1 Clear strength: "One of the things I do best"
- ☐ 2 Hidden strength: "Others rate me higher than I do"
- ☐ 3 Blind spot: "I rate myself higher than others do"
- ☐ 4 Weakness: "I don't do this well"
- ☐ 5 Untested area: "I don't know enough to answer this question"
- ☐ 6 Don't know: "I need more feedback"

Do I have a strong appetite for problem solving/trouble shooting?

- ☐ 1 Clear strength: "One of the things I do best"
- ☐ 2 Hidden strength: "Others rate me higher than I do"
- ☐ 3 Blind spot: "I rate myself higher than others do"
- ☐ 4 Weakness: "I don't do this well"
- ☐ 5 Untested area: "I don't know enough to answer this question"
- ☐ 6 Don't know: "I need more feedback"

THE SIXTH 'C' — CHALLENGES

BATTLES WON AND LOST

What are some examples of challenges that you've overcome for/in the firm?

What are your three biggest failures in your career and what have been the key lessons that you've taken from them?

THE SIXTH 'C' — CHALLENGES

BATTLES WON AND LOST

What Health, Stealth & Wealth Challenges do you foresee in your career? (For example stress, political infighting, legislative changes, fee pressure etc) and what will be your measures to combat them?

CHALLENGE	COMBATIVE ACTION TO TAKE
Health *e.g. Hours worked*	
Stealth *e.g. Competitor marketing*	
Wealth *e.g. Static fees*	

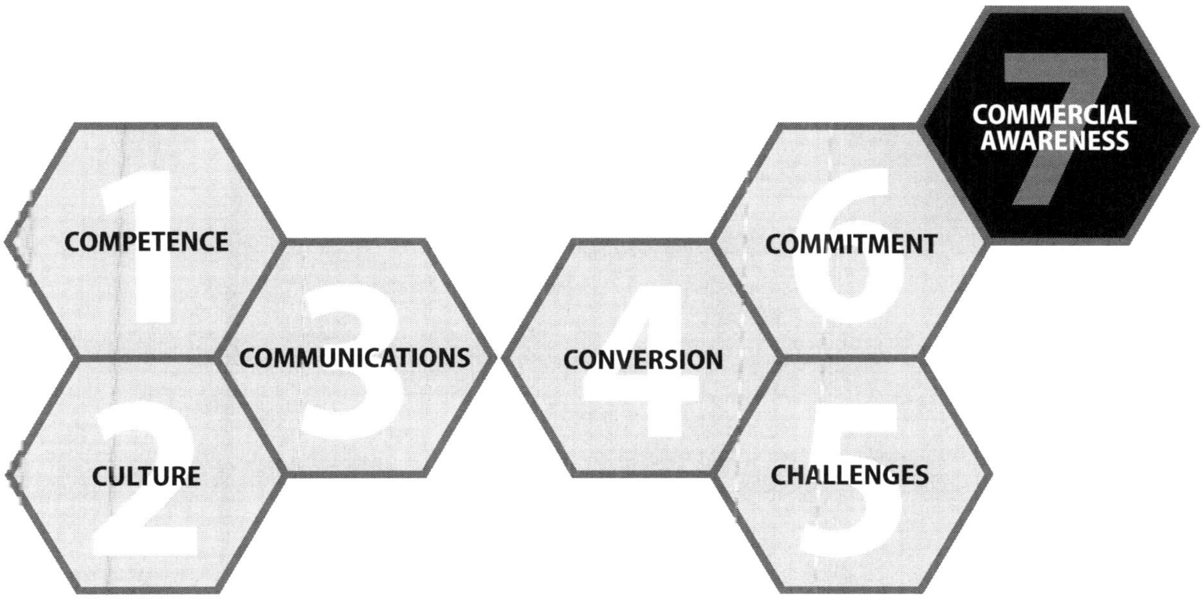

1
COMPETENCE
2
CULTURE
3
COMMUNICATIONS
4
CONVERSION
5
CHALLENGES
6
COMMITMENT
7
COMMERCIAL AWARENESS

THE SEVENTH 'C' — COMMERCIAL AWARENESS

PARTNERSHIP POINTERS

Ask yourself and answer these questions when considering the current and future 'Challenges' behaviours that you'll employ.

1. What is my first reaction to being notified of a client complaint?

2. How well do I understand the role that everyone else plays in the firm, especially the challenges faced by its leadership?

3. Is my focus on making myself look good or solving issues for the firm and its clients as effectively and efficiently as I know how?

THE SEVENTH 'C' — COMMERCIAL AWARENESS

EMPLOYEE VERSUS OWNERSHIP

What makes you think you want to be a Partner?

What makes you think you're good enough to be considered for Partnership in your firm?

What was the average age that the current Partners reached their positions?

What types of challenges do they go through each day as a Partner?

THE SEVENTH 'C' — COMMERCIAL AWARENESS

EMPLOYEE VERSUS OWNERSHIP

What are the biggest lessons they've learned in their time as a Partner of the firm?
(Hint: invite them out to lunch to ask for their advice, counsel, direction and opinion)

What does the Partner you speak to the most think you lack before becoming Partner 'material'?

How long are you prepared to wait to be considered for Partnership before evaluating your options?

How did the Partner you speak to the most get their chance to move up in the firm?

ABOUT MARTIN BISSETT

Martin Bissett is the Founder of The Upward Spiral Partnership Ltd. (USP), the UK-based consulting firm that specialises in the implementation of professional selling and leadership skills in the next generation of accounting professionals.

Previously, Martin served ten years on the board of the directors of the UK's leading provider of high-quality new business appointments for accountancy firms. There, he held the responsibility for the nurture and organic growth of the organisation's new client base, including six of the UK's top 30 firms of accountants.

Martin became fascinated by the apparent juxtaposition of partners not vocalising what they were looking for in terms of an accomplished skill set from their potential future partners and their managers not asking to discover what that skill set included, despite wanting to reach that very position. In a profession with a supposed "Succession Crisis" on the horizon, this apparent "stand off" struck him as curious.

This has led Upward Spiral Partnership to personally interview several hundred partners and managers in the US and UK to learn what partners are looking for and how the managers see their own future in the firm. There are, of course, firms who have addressed this issue already, and their initiatives have also been captured.

The results of the research, including both the consensus and the exceptions to the general opinion, is called "Passport to Partnership." This study provides the highlights of each factor that the majority of partners interviewed use as their criteria when evaluating whether someone in their organisation can make it to the top.

As a result of the combination of his experience, intellectual property and this proprietary research, Martin now consults with accounting firms in the UK, Europe and the USA to support them in their transition through to the next stage of their development and growth.

Tel: +44 077 0892 2622
Email: martin@upwardspiralpartnership.co.uk
Website: http://www.martinbissett.com
LinkedIn: https://www.linkedin.com/in/martinbissett

CPATrendlines

ACTIONABLE INTELLIGENCE FOR THE
TAX, ACCOUNTING & FINANCE COMMUNITY

About CPA Trendlines

Tax, accounting and finance professionals worldwide rely on CPA Trendlines to deliver the actionable intelligence they need to identify and act on emerging issues and opportunities.

We specialize in high-quality, concise executive briefings designed to help busy professionals improve their organizations, advance their careers, and enhance their lives. Our reports are relevant, timely and to-the-point, providing only the most essential, most practical, information. Many are readable in under an hour and are immediately actionable.

Visit us at cpatrendlines.com.

Rick Telberg
President / CEO
CPA Trendlines

21300669R00122

Made in the USA
Middletown, DE
25 June 2015